Managing the Aftermath of Infidelity

This book tackles the challenges that arise from infidelity by helping couples heal through the initial experiences of discovery, providing tools to help partners disclose the details of the affair, manage triggering experiences and obtain forgiveness and reconciliation.

Managing in the Aftermath of Infidelity is organized to speak directly to the betraying partner, the betrayed partner and the therapist independently, offering valuable insights on how each role can assist in making recovery successful. Early chapters direct couples on how to limit potential damage from the fallout of discovery, and subsequent chapters help the couple repair and rebuild a new post-affair relationship. The strategies within this book can be used by the couple alone or as a companion to working with a therapist.

Taking the reader sequentially through the essential steps of affair recovery, this text is an essential guide for marriage counselors and their patients.

Butch Losey is an Assistant Professor at Xavier University, USA and a counselor educator and CEO of a multi-clinician practice in Cincinnati, Ohio. He provides couples counseling for couples recovering from infidelity and other relationship concerns.

Managing the Aftermath of Infidelity

A Sequential Guide for Therapists and Couples

Butch Losey

Routledge
Taylor & Francis Group

NEW YORK AND LONDON

First published 2021
by Routledge
52 Vanderbilt Avenue, New York, NY 10017

and by Routledge
2 Park Square, Milton Park, Abingdon, Oxon, OX14 4RN

*Routledge is an imprint of the Taylor & Francis Group, an
informa business*

© 2021 Taylor & Francis

The right of Butch Losey to be identified as author of this work
has been asserted by him in accordance with sections 77 and
78 of the Copyright, Designs and Patents Act 1988.

All rights reserved. No part of this book may be reprinted
or reproduced or utilised in any form or by any electronic,
mechanical, or other means, now known or hereafter invented,
including photocopying and recording, or in any information
storage or retrieval system, without permission in writing from
the publishers.

Trademark notice: Product or corporate names may be
trademarks or registered trademarks, and are used only for
identification and explanation without intent to infringe.

Library of Congress Cataloging-in-Publication Data
A catalog record for this book has been requested

ISBN: 978-1-138-31777-2 (hbk)
ISBN: 978-1-138-31778-9 (pbk)
ISBN: 978-0-429-45497-4 (ebk)

Typeset in Optima
by SPi Global, India

Contents

Beginning   vii

1   Immediate Actions   1

2   The Dangers in Seeking Support from Family and Friends   13

3   Contact with the Affair Partner   21

4   Lying about the Affair   29

5   The Use of the Polygraph to Detect Lies of the
    Betraying Partner   35

6   Structured Disclosure   43

7   Rebuilding Trust   67

8   Managing Intrusive Thoughts and Images   82

9   Managing Triggering Experiences   93

10 Grieving in Isolation   103

11 The Revenge Variable   110

12 Erotic Recovery   122

13 Reclaiming Strategies   133

14 Acceptance, Forgiveness and Reconciliation   138

Contents

15 Selecting a Therapist for the Two of You   150

16 Ethical and Legal Considerations for Couples Therapy   156

Index   175

Beginning

Well, it finally happened. The affair was discovered, or maybe one of you said, "Enough to all the secrets" and came clean about the affair. Now one of you have purchased this book because you want to try to keep your relationship together. Maybe your partner has given it to you in hopes that it will help you help him or her.

This book is different in a few ways. First, it is written to three audiences; the partner who had the affair, the partner who was hurt by the affair and to the therapist who hopes to help the two of you. Each chapter covers a topic important to recovery and is structured so that each chapter is divided into three sections, one section for each partner and one section for the therapist.

I would suggest that you read this book chapter by chapter, discussing each chapter before proceeding. If working with a therapist or clergy, the three of you can work through the text sequentially to create recovery. I believe that what you are about to read will give you the structure you need in the healing process.

It is important that each chapter has some impact for you personally and relationally. Find a way to translate ideas of the chapter into some form of action. To make that happen, you will need to personally reflect on the material in each chapter and intentionally decide what you will integrate in your daily life. I call this anchoring change. Each chapter will conclude with ideas for anchoring and challenging you to considerable personal, relational and contextual changes.

To anchor change will require a high level of reflection. Again, this needs to be intentional. Read each chapter, reflect deeply on it, reveal your thoughts, feelings and perceptions to your partner and then outwardly express those changes that you want to anchor. Anchoring these concepts is paramount to your success.

Lastly, I will let you in on a personal conflict that I had while writing the book, one that I admit was not comfortably resolved. I wrestled with the language that I use in referring to the person who had the affair versus the person who has been hurt by the affair. How should I address these individuals? "The cheater and the cheated," "The person hurt by the affair" and the "person who had the affair"? As you can see, these titles are either insensitive or cumbersome. I decide on the titles of betrayer and betrayed, first, recognizing that the action of the betrayer has led you to this book and second, that both partners have been hurt in the relationship. I just could not come up with anything better.

A Message for the Betraying Partner

You are the critical component in your partner's healing, particularly early in recovery. One of the early steps is for you to manage the crisis of infidelity and to take charge of your partner's healing. You had the affair, and you need to help heal that trauma for your partner. I call this therapeutic agency. Your "healing presence" will stabilize your partner's lost sense of reality and help stabilize your relationship, setting a foundation for future healing for both of you. Without your help, your partner may not get to a place of forgiveness and reconciliation with you. To create a strong recovery from this, you will need to take the lead in your partner's healing. How you personally manage your partner's pain will matter greatly. Your partner's hurt can be healed with your loving compassion, patience and empathy.

You will need to help your partner have trust in you again. He or she will prefer to maintain a relationship with you only if you can demonstrate that you are a trustworthy person. People tend to think of trust as some endpoint or commodity; it is actually consistency in being a trustworthy person, in multiple contexts and over time. The good news is that consistency in trust-reinforcing behaviors can lead to your partner deciding to stay in the relationship with you. But – and I pause for a moment here for you to take this next statement in – any trust-eroding behaviors on your part will quickly lead to concretizing you as a perpetually untrusting person, adding on additional hurt beyond the trauma of infidelity that will be terribly difficult to heal. Immediately following the discovery of the affair, it is important for you to work hard at being honest, not appearing dishonest, open to sharing the world you kept hidden and open to sharing the world of your thoughts, feelings, perceptions, expectations and yearnings for your relationship.

You will need to confess – without restraint – to what you have done and demonstrate to your partner that you understand the harm caused by your decision to have this affair. Make sure your partner does not have to guess about the affair relationship, the circumstances, the timeline of events or your feelings for the affair partner. I know that this may be really hard to hear as you begin recovery. Your partner does not need to be the investigator; it will only contribute to his or her pain and limit healing.

A Message for the Betrayed Partner

I will be asking your partner to do much of the work during the early part of your recovery. He or she had the affair, and I believe it is his or her responsibility to create stability and trust. Once your relationship is stabilized, I will ask both of you to objectively assess your relationship prior to the affair. Your partner will need to understand his or her own personal issues that contributed to deciding to have an affair. As a couple, you will need to understand the negative patterns in the relationship that the two of you co-created, resulting in weakness and vulnerability for the relationship. You will also need to consider how your own personal issues contributed to the vulnerability of the relationship. These are important steps because it will help you identify and repair the underlying personal issues and relational conditions, of which the affair is a symptom. This does not take away any responsibility from your partner, as he or she chose to have the affair; but it does recognize that the affair can be expressing an interaction between personal vulnerabilities of you and your partner, and the affair is a symptom of this dynamic.

Infidelity is a deep wound. It is a traumatic experience like no other. Common experiences of people who are hurt by infidelity are similar to post-traumatic stress. Many people experience intrusive images and thoughts, flashbacks, hypervigilance, strong desire to investigate, avoidance of feelings and panic attacks. You may be experiencing a number of triggering events that leave you feeling out of control, anxious, aggressive or depressed.

As we begin to work together, I will show you a way to assess the level of trauma symptoms and a number of methods to reduce the impact of the trauma. You can't change what happened, but you can change the impact of the experience. I will have you and your partner implement these strategies and reassess regularly until you can see improvement in the symptoms. This will take considerable commitment from your partner, because I want him or her to create a non-triggering environment for you. I will expect your partner to provide you with a high level of understanding and tolerance for the dysregulated experiences that you may have. I will also expect you to practice some of the personal strategies for managing triggering events. If both of you do this work simultaneously, I believe you will be successful in managing the intrusive thinking and the dysregulation that comes with internal and external triggers.

A Message for the Two of You

Infidelity can destroy a relationship, but many couples find the ability to survive the chaos and pain and move through it to a place of healing and growth. For those couples, the post-affair relationship can have a closeness that has not been present in the relationship for a long time, if ever. Couples that have the courage to continue the relationship, in the wake of severe hurt, certainly take the greatest risk and yet can reap the greatest rewards. Your work begins here, in this moment, as you attempt to stay together while one, or both, of you is deeply hurt.

To continue this relationship will require both of you to be intentional in what you do in the days following discovery of the affair. Emotional responding that leads to escalation, lying and dismissing your partner's perceptions, stalking the affair partner or making threats of divorce will only make things worse. Thinking through your actions will be important. Your relationship will need your commitment when your will is weak and your patience is low. Remind yourself that your commitment is to the future relationship that the two of you will have together. What does that couple need you to do today?

I believe your commitment requires you to look beyond the option to separate. If you are keeping your options open to leaving the relationship, it will be difficult to create substantial change. For example, married couples who are considering divorce do not want to share the details of the affair because they fear the information will be used against them later in court. Partners who plan to stay in the relationship through the pain share the details of the affair, knowing that this is what is necessary to create stability and healing.

> *To be humble in a loving relationship is to willingly invite our partner to see what others do not,*
> *our vulnerable inner world where our true essence resides,*
> *so that he or she can know us more deeply, each and every day.*

A loving relationship requires humility. To be humble in a loving relationship is to willingly invite our partner to see what others do not, our vulnerable inner world where our true essence resides, so that he or she can know us more deeply each and every day. Begin today with a commitment to looking inward to gain a better understanding of who you are, and share this inner world with your partner.

A Message for the Therapist

Treating couples recovering from infidelity requires a specific skill set. Many therapists take on couples with limited training in couples therapy and are prepared even less when it comes to treating infidelity. It is important to note that couples therapy for infidelity is different from traditional couples therapy because infidelity treatment has a specific protocol. For example, couples that enter counseling for infidelity are at a high level of crisis, and the therapist should expect to employee a higher degree of crisis response, especially in the early sessions.

A common error that therapists make when treating infidelity is to treat the affair as the sole issue and fail to see how the affair is communicating information about the state of the relationship between the couple. The affair can be seen as representing an attempt to resolve an existing problem in the relationship. Therapists need to recognize this, delve into the context and underlying dynamics of the relationship and match their approach and interventions to the type of infidelity the couple has experienced.

The process of infidelity treatment tends to move through distinct phases. These phases include crisis management, creating understanding of the underlying dynamics in the relationship, treating these conditions and then implementing post-treatment goals. This book follows these phases and addresses specific issues within these time frames. This will be useful because you will be able to assign chapter readings, and activities within the readings, sequentially throughout the treatment process. With the time limitations of hourly sessions, this book will help you augment treatment for the couple by having more in-depth exploration of the issues that you surely will deal with in treatment.

Final Thoughts

My hope is that you will find actionable things to do in every chapter of this book. The chapters are organized so that crisis is managed first, insight and change are addressed second and sustainability of the new relationship is third. After reading each chapter, I would encourage you as a couple to anchor changes by discussing the chapter together and listing things that each of you are going to do. These will be concrete goals for each of you to accomplish.

Out of chaos comes change
and from change
grows a new relationship.

So, take a deep breath, be mindful of your thoughts, feelings and actions, find the compassion that resides in you and let us begin. It will be hard work, but it is worthy work. Many years of providing couples therapy has taught me that out of chaos comes change, and from change grows a new relationship.

Butch Losey

1 Immediate Actions

How you respond to the immediate aftermath of the infidelity is paramount to your ability to recover from such a devastating impact to your relationship. You must consider implementing those things that will create stability in the relationship and make sure not to do things that create even more damage to the relationship. Some things that you might consider doing may at first seem like a good idea but may not seem so good after thoughtful consideration. So read the following items and consider what needs immediate action. All of these are addressed in detail in the upcoming chapters, but I want you to consider now what you should be doing immediately and the things you should not be doing.

A Message for the Betraying Partner

End the Affair Relationship Immediately, and Forever

It is best to end the affair relationship quickly with no tapering off. Ending the relationship also needs to be done in the full view and awareness of their partner. No clandestine meetings to say goodbye to get closure, and no phone calls in secret to apologize privately. There is no such thing as closure when it comes to infidelity; one relationship will end, either the primary relationship or the affair relationship. Believing in closure and acting upon it will only make the recovery process more difficult and cause more pain for your partner. End the affair now, and forever, and get on to the important business of helping your partner heal and repairing your relationship.

Stop All Future Contact with the Affair Partner

The affair is over, and you will need to keep it that way. If your affair partner contacts you, don't respond. Block email and phone numbers so that there are no opportunities. Immediately tell your partner of any contact by the affair partner, including accidental contact, attempted contact by the affair partner, or any probable contact, such as phone call hang-ups by unknown numbers. Trust-building will inevitably be broken when there is a delay in communicating, or your partner learns of the contact without being told. Damage only continues and recovery freezes when you have contact with the affair partner.

Take Care of Your Physical Health

This early period right after your partner has found out about your affair is one of the most vulnerable times. With emotions running high, it might be tempting to act out of anger or hurt. Emotional responding can only lead to ongoing damage to the relationship. For this reason, it will be important for you to take care of yourself so that you can manage the emotional weeks and months ahead.

Take Care of Your Mental Health

It will be difficult to help your partner if you are not doing healthy things for yourself. I would suggest that you make sure that you have a regular sleep time and that you consciously eat, even though you may not feel like it. Notice if you are relying too heavily on alcohol or other substances to keep you calm or to numb your feelings. If you believe you have depression or anxiety, arrange to see a clinician, or get the two of you into couples therapy immediately. With couples therapy, not only can the clinician help you relationally, but the clinician can also assist you in reducing depression or anxiety or help you address other mental health concerns.

Do Not Leak Information over Time

One sign that you are struggling with making the decision to disclose is when you leak out information over time. There are a number of reasons why you may be consciously or unconsciously leaking out information over time. It may be that you are worried about the negative reaction from your partner or that you are trying to stop the damage that is occurring. It is important if you are lying or "leaking" that you stop so that trust can begin to be re-established.

Disclose Details about Your Affair

One of the early decisions you will need to make is how will you go about disclosing all of the details about your affair. Fair warning here: Not all clinicians agree on if you should disclose all the details of the affair. My take on this is that if you plan to stay together, then disclosing details about your affair has the benefits of re-establishing trust, creating emotional stability for your partner, and it reduces investigating behaviors and intrusive thinking for your partner. As you begin to disclose the details, follow the guidelines in the following chapter on disclosure.

Answer Questions

Asking questions is a big part of making meaning for your partner. When asked a question, answer; when asked the same question again, answer. The rule here would be to show your willingness to answer questions and answer them as best you can. Also, answer similar or redundant questions without irritation and be expansive as possible in your responses. Make sure your responses include information about your behaviors, your thoughts and your feelings.

Take a non-defensive approach to answering questions, even with questions that have been repeatedly asked. Try to move your answers beyond "yes" and "no." Any sign of defensiveness could lead your partner to believe that he or she is not worth the trouble for you to answer the questions.

Do Everything You Can to Prove You Are a Trusting Partner

Consider the behaviors that you need to demonstrate for your partner to trust you. I would suggest that you tell your partner the specific things that you will be doing so that the behaviors can be observed and assessed. Trust is contextual and temporal. Your partner is likely to trust you in some settings more than others. Let your partner know the specific behaviors that you will be doing in the settings that you are least trusted in. Staying consistent in your efforts will lead to increased trust over time.

Trust if afforded to trustworthy people. This means that there are common characteristics of a trusting partner. These include honesty, integrity, accountability and accessibility. When your partner consistently witnesses you being accountable and accessibly, you are perceived as more trustworthy. Accountability and accessibility are specifically critical in the early days after discovery, so let's look at those in more detail.

You will need to work hard so that you can account for all of your time when you are away from your partner. When schedules change or irregularities in schedules occur, immediate disclosure will be important. When this is done well, there is less opportunity for emotional dysregulation for your partner.

You should also be accessible to your partner. On one level, you need to be accessible if your partner needs to get in touch with you. Explanations of poor cell phone reception, cell phone batteries that have died, or situations of not answering text and email messages create strong alarm reactions for your partner. Charging up phones, attending to messages, avoiding poor-reception locations, and offering regular contact when away can make all the difference in establishing accountability and accessibility and ultimately stability and trust. On a deeper level, you will need to be accessible with your heart and mind, maintaining open communication and sharing your internal world to your partner.

Create Protected Time

Be intentional to create protected time. Create regular time with your partner to talk about your affair and for your partner to ask questions. Also create protected time where you enjoy each other and do not talk about the affair. Both are important for your recovery.

Intervene with Triggering Events

What triggers your partner? Is it a scene on a television show? Driving by a specific location? It can be extremely helpful for you to know the primary triggers your partner is experiencing and the early warning signs of the triggers (anxiety, stomach pains, agitation, shortness of breath). Knowing this, the two of you can decide on specific actions for preventing triggers and intervening when early warning signs are present or triggers happen. Couples that create an environment that manages this well ultimately create a supportive environment where triggers are discussed openly and managed with caring behaviors.

> *There is a storm on deck; I am a battered wreck,*
> *I need a calm cove with calm water.*
> —Lindsay, former client

Seek Support from People Who Support the Relationship

You are going through a very private crisis, and you may feel that you have no one to talk to. Be careful in selecting someone supportive to talk to. It is easy for people to take your side, and this may not be helpful if you are trying to save your relationship. Choose someone who supports the two of you; they may be more objective.

A Message for the Betrayed Partner

Take Care of Your Physical Health

I mentioned this earlier to your partner that this early period right after discovery of your partner's affair is one of the most vulnerable times. With emotions running high, it might be tempting to act out of anger or hurt. Emotional responding can only lead to ongoing damage to the relationship. For this reason, it will be important for you to take care of yourself so that you can manage the emotional weeks and months ahead.

Take Care of Your Mental Health

You may feel like your world is on fire right now. In the chaos, you may feel less like eating and have trouble sleeping. You may even recognize that you are not eating and sleeping. Don't allow this to happen. Make an intentional effort to eat and sleep on regular intervals. Eat small, even though you may not even want to eat at all.

Notice if you are relying too heavily on alcohol or other substances to keep you calm or to numb your feelings. If you believe you have depression or anxiety, arrange to see a clinician or get the two of you into couples therapy immediately. With couples therapy, not only can the clinician help you relationally, but the clinician can also assist you in reducing depression or anxiety or help you address other mental health concerns.

Manage Triggering Experiences and Reduce Ruminating

A trigger in its basic form is simply a signal of some sort that leads to a dramatic change in behavior, mood or thinking. In relationship to infidelity, this signal takes you back to the vulnerable, "danger" state when you learned about the affair. These signals can come from internal or external experiences. Some behaviors associated with triggering are investigating, repetitive questioning, intrusive thinking, hypervigilance, ruminating, startle response and escalation. In the upcoming chapters, I will discuss multiple strategies to help with triggering responses for you to do and for both of you to do together.

Present Questions to Solicit Ongoing Discussion

You need information about the affair, and your goal is to get as much information as you can to make sense of things. To keep the conversation going, you will need to ask questions that are not attacking and do not increase defensiveness. When answers are provided, it will be important to try to have your partner expand the answer and to resist discounting it. It may be better to ask another question than to discount the answer. Remember that your goal is to keep your partner disclosing more information and not shutting down, so your questioning will need to be intentional and your approach to your partner's answers needs to be curious, not discounting.

Manage Your Emotions

Emotional regulation for both of you creates the likelihood that you will have more open and productive discussions and much better decision making. The more regulated that you can be, the more likely you will be able to have conversations about intimate and difficult content, which will need to happen frequently as you create understanding about the affair and work to heal your relationship.

Making Emotion-Based Decisions

In the first days of learning about the infidelity, emotional experiences for both of you are intense. Sometimes couples make decisions in the context of this emotional intensity and can cause long-lasting consequences. Emotionally charged decisions about separating, moving out, divorce, and telling the children about the infidelity can have unintended consequences. I would ask you to postpone major decisions long enough to work through the initial crisis with each other or with a trained clinician.

Limit Disclosure of the Affair to Friends, Family and Coworkers

Discovering your partner's affair can be an isolating, lonely experience, and it is certainly important to seek support, but careful selection of the supportive person is important.

Resist the temptation to tell family members how hurt you are by the affair. Telling your partner's parents about their son or daughter's affair without having thought that through as a couple could lead to fracturing the relationship between you and your partner's parents. Any decision to tell others would be best made by the two of you and when emotions are low.

The Affair Partner Is Not a Good Source of Information

The affair partner does not operate on the same value of justice that you do. They will not answer your question because "it is the right thing to do." Thinking that they will answer honestly will likely turn out to be an error in judgment on your part about the affair partner. In all probability, the answers (which may or may not be true) will either hurt you or lead you to more doubt about your partner's story.

Unlike your partner, the affair partner will have no interest in healing their relationship with you or helping you understand the affair, what they talked about, how your partner felt about them, or what kind of sex they had. The affair partner is interested in preserving their positive image, protecting their world from your intrusion and limiting the impact of their affair on their life, preserving the belief that you are the crazy one, getting you to "just go away," limiting your escalation and hiding the truth of their immoral behavior, to name a few. I know this sounds harsh, but I have seen the scenario over and over again. Save yourself some heartache by not contacting the affair partner.

You Do Not Need to Be the Deliverer of Justice

Doing things because they feel good is not always a good decision. Calling the affair partner's spouse can harm another family as it has harmed you. Careful consideration is needed here. Yes, the affair partner's spouse has the right to know, but are you they one who should do that? I think your efforts and energy could be better used on the work in your relationship. In addition, any contact with the affair partner or their partner raises the risk of their involving the legal process, such as a calling the police or seeking a protection order.

A Message for the Therapist

Couples therapy is different from individual therapy. Infidelity treatment is different from couples therapy. To offer treatment for couples experiencing the aftermath of infidelity, you will need to follow a specific protocol for treatment. Infidelity treatment approaches work couples through a process of stabilizing the crisis, helping the couple understand the infidelity and what it is telling the couple about the relationship, treatment of the underlying problematic dynamics of the relationship, facilitating a process of forgiveness and planning prevention strategies. Following is an outline of a protocol for infidelity treatment and some of the common issues that clinicians will need to address. Therapy starts with crisis stabilization.

Crisis Stabilization and Assessment

The beginning efforts of crisis stabilization is creating psychological safety for the couple to take interpersonal risks in session. Your personal presence is key to this. Knowing yourself and staying calm in the presence of chaos is required. There are a couple of tasks that support safety and trust. First, you will need to control the intense emotions of the sessions. Second, you will need to productively discuss the infidelity with the couple. Third, you will need to prepare the couple for therapy by providing a conceptual model for treatment. It is important to do this by the end of the first session. The couple should leave understanding the stages of treatment and the goals and benchmarks for each stage.

You should not forget that the turmoil of infidelity can be accompanied by mental health concerns such as depression, anxiety, suicide ideation, revenge fantasies and aggressive behavior. Many of these mental health concerns are not uncommon; for example, people experiencing infidelity and other "humiliating marital events" are six times more likely to be diagnosed with a major depressive episode than the general population (Cano & O'Leary, 2000). Considering infidelity specifically, people who discover their partner was having an affair are nine times more likely to experience a major depressive episode than the general population (Whisman, 2016).

Suicidal thought should be considered in every case. In a recent study looking at suicide predictors, researchers found that infidelity was the highest predictor for suicide attempts in married women, more so than being threatened with physical assault by their spouse and the number of previous attempts.

Rage and revenge fantasies (toward both the affair partner and the spouse) are also an early experience of the hurt partner, and the client's ability to contain them must be assessed. At times, couples have reported to me that they wish to inflict as much pain on the affair partner as they have experienced. Sometimes the pain they want to inflict is meant to disrupt the life of the affair partner by informing their spouse. Other times they want to inform the spouse because they believe it is morally correct to inform the spouse. Sometimes it is just fantasy, and other times it is not. Some simple questions can reveal a lot. In my book, *Bullying, Suicide and Homicide* (Losey, 2011), I talk about the "triple P" of threat assessment, which are three topic areas that can be discussed to reveal the level of risk for violence toward the affair partner. First is *persistence*. When a high-intensity, elevated mood is persistent over time, it is considered elevated risk. Second is *plausibility*. If the threat is plausible and has detail, it is considered elevated risk. Lastly is *preparation*. If there is evidence of moving from fantasy to action, this would be considered higher risk. When the clinician assesses that there is a genuine concern for the affair partner, the clinician should take action to protect this person, following local law and professional ethics.

Alcohol use adds another level of challenge for recovery and can exacerbate existing conditions such as depression and anxiety. Alcohol and substance use increase poor decision-making that can lead to continuation or impulsive connection to the affair partner, higher levels of conflict with their spouse or suicide ideation.

I frequently offer three-hour intensive sessions for couples. During my first intensive session with a couple, I briefly ask the couple to assess their relational crisis in categories of boundaries. These boundaries are discussed in the upcoming chapters. Table 1.1 outlines my guide to screening boundaries.

There are a number of free-access measures for depression, anxiety and substance use. These may be helpful as you help the couple sort out boundaries and work to create stability. The following is a short list of these free-access measures; most of these were presented at the All Ohio Counselor Conference in Columbus Ohio (Erford, 2012).

- The Hamilton Rating Scale for Depression
- The Center for Epidemiologic Studies Depression Scale
- Zung Self-Rating Depression Scale
- Generalized Anxiety Disorder Screener
- Zung Self-Rating Anxiety Scale
- Hamilton Anxiety Screener
- Michigan Alcohol Screening Test (MAST)
- Alcohol Use Disorders Identification Test (AUDIT)

Table 1.1 Boundary Guide

Trauma symptoms	
	Intrusive thoughts and images
	Investigating
	Triggering events
Leakage and lying	
	Leaking out information over time
Protect time and personal presences in the relationship	
Boundaries with others	
	Contact with the affair partner
	Contact with the affair partner's spouse
	Discussions with family and friends
	Legal system and protection orders
Physical health self-care	
Commitment expectations	
	Commitment to the relationship
	Commitment to therapy
Relationship expectations	
Trust	
	Trust-building behaviors
	Characteristics of a trusting partner
Mental health	
	Depression and anxiety
	Suicide thought and revenge fantasies
	Substance abuse
Other triangulating issues	
	Pornography
	Work
	Friend group
Communication	
Disclosure	

Bibliography

Cano, A., & O'Leary, K. D. (2000). Infidelity and separations precipitate major depressive episodes and symptoms of nonspecific depression and anxiety. *Journal of Consulting and Clinical Psychology*, 68(5), 774–781.

Cramer, R. E., Abraham, W. T., Johnson, L. M., & Manning-Ryan, B. (2001). Gender differences in subjective distress to emotional and sexual infidelity: Evolutionary or logical inference explanation? *Current Psychology*, 20(4), 327–336.

Erford, B. (2012). *Free access assessment instruments for depression, anxiety, eating disorders, disruptive behavior and substance use. All Ohio Counselor Conference*, Columbus, Ohio.

Frederik, D. A., & Fales, M. R. (2016). Upset over sexual versus emotional infidelity among gay, lesbian, bisexual and heterosexual adults. *Archive of Sexual Behavior*, 45, 175–191.

Geary, D. C., Rumsey, M., Bow-Thomas, C. C., & Hoard, M. K. (1995). Sexual jealousy as a facultative trait: Evidence from the pattern of sex differences in adults from China and the United States. *Ethology and Sociobiology*, 16, 355–383.

Losey, B. (2011). *Bullying, Suicide, and Homicide: Understanding, Assessing, and Preventing Threats to Self and Others for Victims of Bullying*. New York: Routledge.

Rahmani, F., Salmasi, S., Rahmani, F., Bird, J., Asghari, E., Robai, N., Jafarabadi, M. A., & Gholizadeh, L. (2018). Domestic violence and suicide attempts among married women: A case–control study. *Journal of Clinical Nursing*, 28, 3252–3261.

Sabini, J., & Green, M. C. (2004). Emotional responses to sexual and emotional infidelity: Constants and differences across genders, samples, and methods. *Personality and Social Psychology Bulletin*, 30(11), 1375–1388.

Shackelford, T. K., LeBlanc, G. J., & Drass, E. (2000). Emotional reactions to infidelity. *Cognition and Emotion*, 14(5), 643–659.

Urooj, A., & ul-Haque, A. (2015). Perception of emotional and sexual infidelity among married men and women. *Pakistan Journal of Psychological Research*, 30(2), 421–439.

Whisman, M. A. (2016). Discovery of a partner affair and major depressive episode in a probability sample of married or cohabiting adults. *Family Process*, 55(4), 713–723.

The Dangers in Seeking Support from Family and Friends

As I write this, I am aware that I will probably sound like an alarmist, but I write this as a cautionary prelude to you sharing your pain with someone. The weeks after discovery of an affair can be an isolating, lonely experience for both of you, and it is certainly important to seek support, but careful selection of the supportive person is important.

I am sure that on many occasions in the past you have found it helpful to talk about other stressful events with a close friend, family member or someone close at work. The infidelity that occurred in your relationship can be a very different matter. I have worked with many couples that have selected "supportive" friends and family to talk to without ever considering if it is truly a wise choice. Hopefully in this chapter I will convey that any of your family and friends can be of great support to you, and that it is important to take a little time considering the vulnerabilities in those relationships.

The challenge with seeking support from others is knowing what kind of support you will get and what kind you want. If you are considering rebuilding your relationship after the affair, you will need to select someone who supports and loves you and also supports the continued recovery of the relationship. If you are considering separation, selecting a support person who has your best interest in mind makes sense.

It is hard for people to recognize that you may want support for the relationship and will immediately jump to supporting only what is best for you. If the intent is to stay together, make it clear to your family and friends that you are planning to stay together and that part of the help you need is feedback about what might be in the best interest of the relationship, which may squarely sit in your blind spot.

An obvious unbiased support person would be a therapist. I would recommend a couples therapist who can work with the two of you. If you seek a therapist for individual counseling, you will run the same risk of the therapist supporting only you unless you request that they help you with getting feedback for the benefit of the relationship.

Timing of Talking with Others

The early instability following affair discovery means that all of your options are on the table, including anger, aggression, retribution, divorce, understanding, empathy and reconciliation. Your early response choices may be to lash out or to make threats of divorce, but later your decision may be to work for reconciliation and forgiveness with your partner. Because of this instability, telling anyone about your partner's infidelity – or, possibly, your infidelity – should be carefully weighed against their flexibility in accepting your changing decisions.

Consider Melanie and Dave, a couple I saw a few years ago, who started meeting with me a week after discovery of the affair. Dave had the affair, and when Melanie discovered it, she talked with her mother, Joan, for support. Melanie confided to Joan that she likely planned to leave Dave and file for divorce. Joan supported her and helped her find an attorney. A few days later, Melanie and Dave had a long conversation, and the couple decided to stay together, attend counseling and work to save their marriage. Joan was less than enthusiastic. She immediately began to doubt if her daughter was being rational and challenged Melanie to reconsider her decision, creating considerable conflict between mother and daughter. Melanie and Dave did the hard work of therapy, and Melanie was able to forgive Dave. The couple developed a strong relationship with one another and the couple stayed together. After some time, Joan and Melanie were also able to repair their relationship, but Joan was unable to forgive Dave and had little trust for him following his affair.

The danger in early sharing about infidelity in your relationship is that your decisions about the relationship may change over time. Your family and friends may not be as flexible as you are with your changing decisions. You also have to consider that your capacity to forgive may be greater than that of others, and others may never be able to forgive. Your capacity to forgive strengthens, particularly if you are in therapy, because therapy requires significant work from both of you toward forgiveness and reconciliation. Others will not have the same opportunity to experience that with you or know all the details that will come to light about the affair and what contributed to it.

A Message for the Betraying Partner

As you seek out assistance and support from others, keep in mind that it is critically important to keep an open avenue of communication with your partner. It may be very confusing for your partner because your partner may have anger toward you and are deeply hurt by you, and your partner may also have empathy for you and want to understand. Early conversations about how you can support your partner may also lead to conversations about support for you and whether or not the support comes in part from your partner, family member, friend, clergy, therapist or someone the two of you agree on who would be helpful to you.

Dangers in Talking with Your Partner's Family

You may have a good, intimate relationship with your partner's family. Sometimes, these good relationships are not tested with strong adversity. Tough conversations may have been avoided in the past, and this has helped reduce conflict with your partner's family. Of course, if your part-ner's family is reactionary, you will need to be careful in what you share.

One potential reaction to learning about your infidelity is that your partner's family may unexpectedly lash out at you in anger because you have hurt their son or daughter, sister or brother, and they may feel com-pelled to protect your partner from further hurt. This will make it less likely that they will support your relationship.

Another danger in disclosing that you had an affair is that your affair may confirm hidden assumptions that your partner's family had about you, whether true or not, and they may then voice those assumptions from a perspective of pain, which will make it difficult to recover.

Dangers in Talking with Your Best Friend

Considerable concealment has occurred as you engaged in your affair. Your friend may have been a party to the crime and may not have clear objectivity as you work to heal the relationship. Even if your friend did not have direct involvement in the concealment of the affair or help in your connection with the affair partner, they may have turned a blind eye to the situation. If this is the case, it suggests that they are not completely supportive of your relationship with your partner. It might therefore be wise to seek support from someone else.

Dangers in Talking with Your Partner's Best Friend

Talking to your partner's friend may put the friend in a bind in that they may be uncomfortable hearing information about your affair or the intimate aspects of your relationship. What you share with this friend may not have been disclosed by your partner and could be considered a breach of trust.

Talking to this friend may also appear that you are seeking alliance with the best friend. If you choose not to disclose to your partner that you are talking to this person and you are discovered, it may increase the hurt in the relationship and fracture your partner's friendship with this person, potentially forever.

Dangers in Talking with One of Your Partner's Friends

This might spell trouble if this person has had interest in you in the past. Intimate conversations can be risky and could be misconstrued. You also need to be careful that you are not selecting this person because of some unexpressed attraction that you have for this person that may work to triangulate the relationship with your partner instead of support it.

We all gossip. Even when we say we won't. You risk this friend telling your story to some or all of your friend network.

Dangers in Talking with Your Children

I do not support telling the children under the age of 18 that one partner had an affair. Your relationship with your partner is private to the two of you. You may not always have a relationship with your partner, but the two of you will always be their mother and father. Telling the children that your relationship is ending or in trouble is hard enough. Telling the kids that you had an affair adds an additional layer of complexity, which may be out of their ability to understand and may be very difficult for them to overcome and forgive.

The risk in discussing your infidelity with your adult children is that you might inadvertently, or maybe even purposefully, demean your partner. Your children possibly do not want to hear how bad your partner has behaved and may not want to hear the details of what has been going on in your relationship.

For Reflection …
Who supports you *and* wants your relationship to succeed?

A Message for the Betrayed Partner

Dangers in Talking with Your Partner's Family

You may have a great relationship with someone in your partner's family, yet confiding in them could lead to outright denials by family members who can't fathom that their brother, sister, daughter or son could do such a thing. They may insist that you are misreading your partner's intent or exaggerating things. The affair behaviors you are describing of your partner may not match how family members have historically perceived your partner, so they may even outright reject your perceptions. This will add insult to injury, and you may learn to resent his or her family because they chose to stick up for your partner instead of supporting you.

Dangers in Talking with Your Best Friend

Other than your partner, your best friend is probably the person that you confide in the most. With many of the couples that I work with, it is sometimes the best friend who should have been considered a suspect all along. The cheating best friend has insider information to your relationship, listens and knows your suspicions and can be very effective at helping keep the infidelity a secret from you. So, early discussion with your best friend about suspicions that you have about your partner could give ammunition for strengthening secrecy.

A young man I worked with suspected that his golf buddy (Todd) was having an affair with his girlfriend, Melissa, because Todd was sleeping around with other women. Todd also had a close relationship with Melissa. He never told his friend he suspected him but talked frequently about his fears that Melissa was having an affair with someone. Todd would tell him he was being paranoid and then later would share the information with Melissa. I know this sounds terrible, but make absolutely sure that your best friend is not the affair partner. Your best friend could have their own secrets.

Dangers in Talking with Your Partner's Best Friend

Your partner's best friend is not your best friend. This person's alliance is with your partner, not you. This friend may lie to protect your partner, and even if they stop the lying and protection, it can complicate things more. An initial lie to you will make it difficult for you to trust this person ever again.

Dangers in Talking with One of Your Partner's Friends

One of your partner's friends may have been waiting in the wings to connect with you. Now that your relationship is in trouble, they may take advantage of your vulnerability by cloaking their true motive behind expressions of support for your troubled relationship. It may be very difficult to distinguish between support of someone in your friend network and what may actually be a play on your vulnerability.

Dangers in Talking with Your Children

I do not support telling the children under the age of 18 that one partner had an affair. Your relationship with your partner is private to the two of you. You may not always have a relationship with your partner, but the two of you will always be their mother and father. Telling the children that your relationship is ending or in trouble is hard enough. Telling the kids that you had an affair adds an additional layer of complexity, which may be out of their ability to understand and may be very difficult for them to overcome and forgive.

The risk in discussing your partner's infidelity with your adult children is that you might inadvertently, or maybe even purposefully, demean your partner. Early conversations with adult children tend to be clouded in anger and shock, and you may be less likely to filter what you share. Your children possibly do not want to hear how bad your partner has behaved and may not want to hear the details of what has been going on in your relationship.

For Reflection …
Who supports you *and* wants your relationship to succeed?

A Message for the Therapist

If you have the opportunity to meet with the couple within the first day or two of discovery or disclosure, you could have a significant impact on limiting damage that can come from the partners' hastily seeking support from family and friends and sharing information about the affair with others. A key component will be your ability to help the couple assess the risks and benefits of sharing with others, coupled with doing this early in treatment. A number of dangers need to be considered before the couple considers sharing personal information about their relationship problems, and I review these with the partners. If possible, you should work to help the couple negotiate and come to agreement about who is appropriate to seek support. Problems occur when one partner chooses to talk to a friend about the affair without consulting the other partner or does not evaluate the risk of sharing. You can be quite helpful in offering guidance and predicting positive outcomes for wisely choosing supportive friends and family.

Assessing the Quality of Support from Others

From a systemic perspective, I first evaluate the quality of support based on what best serves the relationship. I would encourage support from individuals that promote the recovery of the relationship, not necessarily what is best for one partner over the relationship. For example, if a friend is a strong protective support for one of the partners, the friend might suggest separation for a period of time for the partner to take care of themselves. Separation may be contrary to the ongoing work that is needed between the two partners, both in session and out of session. The fire is hot now, and out of the crisis may come significant understanding and change. If the couple is never together, this opportunity may not materialize or may be delayed considerably. In addition, my hope is to move the couple closer to one another in understanding and connection with the crisis, not to make the couple more distant.

There are other considerations that I focus on to help the couple assess potential supportive individuals. First and foremost, like therapy, it would be helpful if the person had the ability to offer empathy and understanding of the pain of infidelity and be able to separate from their own relational history of hurts. Trust is a foundation to support, and the person needs to be trustworthy and have the ability to maintain confidentiality. The boundaries need to be set with this person and just not assumed. Lastly, the person should be objective and understand that there are multiple contributions to infidelity. This will also align with the systemic support for recovery of the relationship.

Be careful recommending individual counseling for one or both partners while in treatment with you. Participation in individual therapy while also attending couples therapy is a highly risky way to try to resolve couple distress, often promoting relationship breakup. I have seen this in my practice. In a majority of the cases, I found that it was not as productive as I had hoped, and I discontinued the practice of referring people to individual counseling while in couples therapy. If individual counseling is needed, it is usually due to severe psychopathology, intimate partner violence or addictions. I will temporarily suspend couples counseling and have one or both partners complete individual counseling before returning to couples counseling. To me, it sounds like a messy prospect to have three therapists involved in a couples case (one for the couple treatment and one for each partner to work with individually).

3 Contact with the Affair Partner

Contact with the affair partner presents challenges for your recovery as a couple. Certainly, ongoing contact with the affair partner by the betraying partner will continue the hurt, dysregulation and fear for the betrayed partner. Yet, many betrayed partners consider meeting with the affair partner to interrogate, investigate or gain perspective. In my experience, others have even met as a couple with the affair partner and even the affair partner's spouse. Some contact unfortunately escalates to stalking, violence and arrest of the betrayed partner.

A Message for the Betraying Partner

It is important that you end contact with the affair partner. The relationship with the affair partner is a triangulating relationship. Someone told me once that the affair relationship kept him married. Sounds horrible, correct? What he meant by this is that having the affair kept the marriage in limbo and he stayed unhappily married, but the conflict reduced a bit, although it simmered. This is triangulation. When you triangulate, you invest energy into a third relationship, taking power away from your primary relationship. The effect is that it will potentially freeze some of the conflict, yet it will also freeze the growth and intimacy in the relationship. If you continue contact with the affair partner, you continue to triangulate the primary relationship, freezing it in place, with no growth or recovery. You need to stop the contact immediately if you plan to heal this relationship.

As you consider how to pull your relationship back together, I would like you to consider a few myths that people hold about the affair relationship.

The Myth of Meeting to Say Goodbye

A thought may be going through your mind: "We should meet one last time to say goodbye. Once we say goodbye, I will have closure, [he or she] will have closure." Though it may sound like a healthy thing to do, I personally believe you are deceiving yourself. Meeting with the affair partner to say goodbye creates added risk and temptation for you and can level a new harm to your partner.

Whatever you are searching for in this person, or searching for in yourself, can be better discovered as you turn back toward your partner and address the issues you allowed to fester in your relationship. Doing this work will bring both of you to a better place of emotional and relational health. The alternative is moving from relationship to relationship, perpetuating destructive patterns and not maturing in a relationship.

The Myth of Falling in Love

Poets and songwriters have described the concept of love through the millennia. It is a deeply evolving experience. When poets talk about love, they are not talking about an affair relationship. I thought I would take a shot at writing a poem about the "love" that occurs in an affair relationship. It takes on some of the myths that people associate with affair relationships.

Ode to the Affair Partner

I love you because you are not like my spouse;
In truth, others can see,
You are quite similar to she.

You are fun, free and easy with me.
I can't wait to see you;
When we sneak out and are finally free.

I ran to you as I ran from my spouse.
I blame it on her, but it's most certainly "we."
To fix things would be hard, I would rather be free.

You see the good in me, I see the good in you;
We silently ignore all the flaws that we see.

I am pleased to know that you will not see
my failings, my fears and the scars within me.

Our relationship is not burdened
By difficult things.
Like mortgages, children or schedules to meet.

Our love is a secret
because we know it is fraught.
The excitement will last …
Last until we are caught.

The Myth of Loyalty

You might think that you owe something to the affair partner and there-fore you might want to delay severing ties or doing things that make it easier for the affair partner. You are engaging in what I call misplaced loyalty. Your loyalty is to your primary relationship, even with all the faults and struggles it may currently have. As long there is this misplaced loy-alty, damage will occur in your primary relationship. Your affair partner entered into your affair knowing that you were committed elsewhere and took the risk, as you did, that this would end poorly for the affair relation-ship. End the affair quickly and precisely.

For Reflection …
What myths do you ascribe to? What phrase in the poem rings true for you?

A Message for the Betrayed Partner

Contacting the Affair Partner

Contacting the affair partner comes with risks. Contacting the affair part-ner in person is probably the riskiest. If you contact the affair partner in person and without their consent, it increases fear in them and risks for yourself. The affair partner has lots to protect – losing a job, being discovered in an affair, losing friendships and family, and children finding out.

Contacting the affair partner by electronic means can be used for evidence against you in a harassment and stalking case. Repeated contacts can be used to demonstrate a pattern, and it can have worse consequences if the recipient of your contact has asked you to stop and you have not. This could lead to protection orders or criminal complaints.

Contacting the Affair Partner for Information

Maybe your partner is not fully forthcoming in answering your questions. Your hurt coupled with unanswered questions may lead you to considering confronting the affair partner or setting up a meeting to ask questions. I can only think of one occasion when this has worked out for couples in my practice, and even with this situation, there were still several unintended negative consequences for the couple and their family. In most circumstances, contacting the affair partner will not be successful.

Contacting the affair partner to get information about the affair comes with at least a minimum assumption on your part that the person you are contacting will be kind, open and have your best interest in mind. Yet, you know that the affair partner has been a deceitful person in perpetuating the affair and they have many good reasons to continue this behavior, even though they have been caught. They may need to protect their own primary relationship, they may still have interest in your partner, they may want to disrupt your relationship or they may have embarrassment or shame that will keep them from disclosing. So, it is quite possible that they will continue to lie and not be forthcoming. They should never be considered a good source of information, and you would be wise not to base important decisions on the information obtained by the affair partner.

At the other end of the continuum, they may want to stick it to you and tell you way more than you want to know. The information they choose to share with you may also be highly embellished to hurt or offend you. This may include attacking your character or intelligence for not seeing this coming.

Another frustrating experience that you may encounter when contacting the affair partner is that of the affair partner defending your partner and using your relationship in their defense. They might state that your partner is a wonderful person, that your partner still loves you, that they are a great husband/wife/father/mother, and that you should forgive them. They may criticize you or tell you how to be a better partner. Unfortunately, their statements will only leave you with a stronger sense that your partner had an intimate relationship with this person and that your partner has talked to the affair partner about your relationship with your partner, your kids' relationship, and his/her love for you. Any way you mix that, it is not going to leave you feeling too great.

If you contact the affair partner for a fact-finding mission, the discussion may result in the affair partner contradicting your partner's perspective of events (which could be either statements of lies or statements of truths), creating more doubt about what happened between the two of them.

Maybe you have considered secretly contacting the affair partner to get information and then "quizzing" your partner to compare the two stories. I call these "truth snares," and they are meant to catch the betraying partner in a lie. The problem with truth snares is that you would be basing the truth snare on highly suspicious information obtained from the affair partner. It may qualify as a snare but have no truth in it.

Contacting the Affair Partner to Express Hurt

Part of any conversation with the affair partner includes expressing hurt. There are two primary challenges with this. First, the affair partner may not express empathy for what you are going through. This in itself will add to the hurt you are feeling. Second, you may not be able to express the hurt in a way that it can be heard by the affair partner. You might find that when your expressions of hurt are not met with empathy, you will lash out at the affair partner. This will only be met with less empathy and aggression toward you – again adding to your level of hurt.

I believe you should have considerable restraint as you consider contacting the affair partner. Below, I share an email exchange that occurred between Dina, a betrayed partner and my former client, and the affair partner, who I will call Janie. I share it with you so that you can see how easily words can be turned against you and how the contact has only complicated an already hurtful situation. The conversation that follows is similar to many others I have heard about in therapy sessions. I have condensed the conversation and picked it up during the middle of the email exchange.

Janie (affair partner)	I am not trying to cause you any trouble between you and Bill. You have nothing to worry about with me. I have been fighting stage 3 breast cancer and just finished chemo. I just thought you should know so that you will finally understand that I am not a threat. I do not expect a response.

Janie dismisses Dina's concerns, telling her that she is not a threat. Hurt by this statement, Dina escalates the conversation.

Dina	You both should be very proud of yourself for having an affair. I would really like to know if your husband ever found out about it. You both have caused me a lot of grief. I will never forgive you. The only thing I would like to know about you is when I can read your obituary.
Janie (affair partner)	Hopefully for your sake, that will be very soon.

Dina seems to be perpetuating her own pain here. She continues to lash out at Janie and the outcome can only lead to more negative comments from her.

Dina	Why did you think it was necessary to tell me about your health condition? Was this your way of letting me know that you are sorry for what you have done and how you destroyed our marriage? My only regret is that I did not make him leave and go to you, you deserve each other.
Janie (affair partner)	I'm sorry for you in that you are such an angry person. I did not destroy your marriage. If it is destroyed, that is between the two of you. The only reason I sent you the email was to try and convince you that I am not a threat to you and never have been. I don't choose to argue with you or defend myself. I have other things that are much more important.

Janie is disengaging from the conversation, and this would have been a good opportunity for Dina to stop emailing. However, she continues to express her hurt to Janie, and surprisingly, Janie continues the conversation.

Dina
One last question, did you tell your husband about the affair?

Janie (affair partner)
I am not married and there was NO affair to tell about.

Dina
What is your definition of an affair? What do you call hiding behind building having make-out sessions, kissing and groping each other like teenagers, hundreds of text messages, getting a PO box so that you can send cards and whatever through mail?

Now Janie changes her response to deny the affair, deny her behaviors, talk kindly about Bill and talk about the problems in Dina's relationship with Bill. She also offers some marriage advice. None of this will be welcomed or accepted by Dina and actually will be more inflaming and hurtful to hear.

Janie (affair partner)
Bill was a friend. A kind, intelligent human being. There was no sex, no make-out sessions as you call them. Maybe he exaggerated what took place so that he could get YOUR attention and maybe you would treat him like the person he is rather than always making him feel like a failure and not good enough to you. If you truly love your husband, then quit punishing him for something he did NOT do. Be a partner and treat him as an equal. I will have my attorney send you a copy of the obituary so that you can have your celebration.

For Reflection …

How strong is your desire to contact the affair partner? What do you hope to gain from this contact? What other ways can you get this need without contacting the affair partner?

27

A Message for the Therapist

I tend to take a strong perspective when couples are talking about contacting the affair partner. I think it is important to challenge the myth that it will be a helpful experience. Yes, I have on rare occasions heard that it was somewhat helpful, but even then, it resulted in more questions and hurt feelings more than it offered answers and healing.

Recovery is going to require your couple to direct the energy back toward each other. The triangulated relationship had all of its energy outward, and it has kept the couple from addressing the problems within their relationship. Strong boundaries will need to be set to give recovery its best chance.

Ongoing contact between the betraying partner and the affair partner perpetuates the triangulation in the relationship and damages the safety needed for the betrayed partner. There is an immediate need for the betraying partner to end the affair relationship and focus efforts on the primary relationship. The betraying partner needs to end the problematic alliance with the affair partner.

"Planned contact" that is agreed upon by the betrayed partner and the affair partner creates additional instability, even though on the surface it appears that the affair partner is willingly helpful. However, it can be hard to tell what the motivation is for the affair partner. Is it to settle things and share as little as possible? Is it to set the record straight on the affair partner's view of the primary relationship? One poorly constructed comment or question can lead to an incredibly hurtful exchange.

This contact also allows the affair partner to continue to influence the relationship in a negative way. Information will be presented as facts; new information will be offered without regard for its impact on the relationship. Confusion will result from trying to decipher what to believe, and conflict will increase when the betraying partner refutes the information. Therapy is delayed by trying to sort out all the mess.

"Confrontational contact" between the affair partner and the betrayed partner is even more dangerous. The affair partner has lots to protect. The betrayed partner poses extreme risks to livelihood and personal relationship, and confrontational contact could lead to violence or legal action.

I suggest encouraging your couple to get their focus off the affair partner and onto their own recovery. This will be more productive.

4

Lying about the Affair

I know this will not come as a surprise to you, but lying is a common strategy when someone is discovered having an affair. Most times, the lies are meant to limit damage as the person attempts to figure out how to manage the discovery. Unfortunately, the reverse occurs; it causes long-term consequences. This is why I recommend that, if couples want to preserve their primary relationship, the person involved in the affair should "come clean" immediately and tell their partner what they have been doing.

A Message for the Betraying Partner

What Constitutes a Lie?

Take time to consider if any of these types of lies are in play in your relationship right now. The first type of lie is a lie of commission. This is the direct lie. Most people understand this clearly. This type of lie is a false statement made knowingly and deliberately.

The second type of lie is a lie of omission. A deliberate omission can be considered a lie if the lack of information alters the outcome. If the withholding of information changes your partner's judgment in some way, then it is a lie. The third type of lie is a lie of influence, sometimes called a character lie. These statements are meant to put the focus on the person lying and away from the truth, to make the liar seem like a good person. For example, the person lying might say "for the fifteen years we have been married, I have never purposefully hurt you." This would be a character lie.

For Reflection ...
What would be the positive consequences for telling the truth? How might responding "in truth" change safety, trust, intimacy and emotional stability?

Men Who Lie: What Men Need to Know about Emotional and Sexual Intimacy

It is not uncommon for couples to come to therapy distinguishing between sexual and emotional infidelity. Sometimes the distinction is made to highlight the pain associated with it. Frequently, though, I hear heterosexual men explaining that they "did not have sex with her" and that it was just an emotional connection, even when it is clear later in therapy that the affair relationship was primarily sexual. So, what motivates men to lie about having sex with their affair partner and emphasize that it was just an emotional affair?

Different feelings are associated with sexual and emotional infidelity. In general, sexual infidelity is associated with anger and blame, but emotional infidelity is associated with hurt feelings (Sabini & Green, 2004). It is possible then that men believe that their partner will be hurt if they disclose the emotional aspects of the infidelity and highly angered and blaming if it is discovered that they were sexual. Maybe the thinking is that hurt feelings are easier managed than the blame and anger.

Something else could be going on with men, though, when the lie emphasizes that the affair relationship was only emotional and not sexual. My guess would be that men are thinking from their own perspective and fabricate a lie based on that perspective. For example, he may believe that he would be highly stressed if his partner engaged in a sexual relationship verses an emotional one. Therefore, men may lie by saying that the affair was only emotional in hopes that their partner will be relieved by the news that it was not sexual.

However, there are gender differences in level of distress based on type of infidelity. In research studies using "forced-choice" surveys, men report more distress by sexual infidelity, and women report more distress by emotional infidelity (Urooj & ul-Haque, 2015; Cramer et al., 2001; Shackelford et al., 2000; Geary et al., 1995). This gender difference has been shown to apply to all age groups, income levels, history of being cheated on, history of being unfaithful, relationship type and length of the relationship. The gender differences do not apply, however, to bisexual or gay men and women (Frederik & Fales, 2016).

When men lie and state that the affair was just emotional, when it was truly more of a sexual relationship, it is a misguided strategy and potentially doubly harmful. First, lying when caught in an affair causes long-term consequences to intimacy, trust and integrity. Even small lies and omissions can make recovery from the affair considerably more difficult, if not impossible. I use the term "leakage" to describe the tendency for the caught partner to leak out information over time, and only when confronted with the undeniable truth.

Second, when men emphasize the emotional aspects of the affair as a means of limiting the distress for their female partner, particularly when the relationship was sexual with limited emotional involvement, it may actually cause greater distress for women than just being truthful about the sexual nature of the affair.

A Message for the Betrayed Partner

Why Does the Betraying Partner Lie about the Affair?

You might be telling yourself that your partner is a liar and will always be a liar. If you are basing that belief on your partner's behavior when you discovered their affair, your assumption may not be completely correct. It is possible that your partner lied when discovered and can also be committed to being truthful in the future. Let me share some of the common reasons people lie, and maybe this will offer a different perspective.

I believe that one of the primary reasons people initially lie when discovered in an affair is that they just don't know what to say. It could be that your partner did not know how to put their thoughts into words or appropriately describe what they have done.

Another common reason people lie is for damage control. Your partner may have hoped that repairing the relationship was possible and didn't want to reveal more facts in fear that things will get worse or will cause greater pain for you.

Embarrassment and guilt are also reasons people identify as reasons for lying. Your partner may be so focused on the guilt of having an affair and hurting you that they find it too difficult to talk about.

Lying was wrong, and the truth is what you really need. Discuss the reasons for the lying with your partner for both of you to gain this understanding. What does this mean for your future relationship with each other?

Gaslighting

The term gaslighting is in reference to the 1944 movie *Gaslight*, in which Ingrid Bergman plays a woman whose husband slowly manipulates her into believing that she is going insane. In doing so, he distracts her from his own criminal activities. You can see how the term gaslighting may be described in the context of infidelity. Gaslighting is a fairly common occurrence prior to the discovery of the affair in which the betraying partner attempts to divert the betrayed partner's suspicions and challenge his or her sense of reality. It can evolve to be particularly mean, with the betraying partner calling the betrayed partner crazy, telling the betrayed partner that he or she needs therapy and telling him or her how hurtful their suspicions are, all the while knowing that they are engaged in an affair.

For Reflection ...
What will be the benefit of deep, truthful conversation about the affair? Outline these benefits and consider inviting your partner to discuss these with you. With your partner, identify barriers to being deeply truthful. What agreement can the two of you make about asking and answering questions about the affair?

A Message for the Therapist

Lies happen in therapy. Some are small white lies that have little conse-quence, and yet people do it. Some have significant consequences and it is fairly apparent that the story being promulgated doesn't add up. This is distressing for the betrayed partner. It can also be highly frustrating for the therapist because we are aware of the negative impact of the behavior the lie is meant to protect and the impact to trust that the lie will cause.

In the chapter on using the polygraph, I make the point that it is dif-ficult to detect a lie, even when the detector is a professional. With that in mind, I don't try to assess if someone is lying. I do make observations, encourage perceptions from the partners and offer gentle challenges.

Suspected Lies during Therapy Sessions

Prevention First

Prevention of lying is the starting point, and prevention obviously is best accomplished early on. One way to approach the expectation of truthful-ness is to make the suggestion that people get more out of therapy if they remain open and honest. I will support authentic and congruent expres-sion across sessions, and honesty is just one way to be authentic. I will connect the discussion with other expectations of congruency, such as expressions of thoughts and feelings.

Informed Observations

I will ask the suspected "lying" partner, "What do you think your partner is perceiving that suggests that you might be lying?" I may share my own observations and perceptions. I will also restate that authentic interactions can enhance the therapeutic process.

Gentle Challenge

When I want to be more direct in my response, I will gently challenge statements that appear to be deceptive. I might ask, "Can we talk about why it's hard to talk about that?" I might gently assume that there is something emotionally connected to the potential deception and state,

"I wonder if there are other parts of what you are talking about that are painful or hard to talk about." I may also encourage more discussion by stating "I am wondering if I am missing something."

Bibliography

Cramer, R. E., Abraham, W. T., Johnson, L. M., & Manning-Ryan, B. (2001). Gender differences in subjective distress to emotional and sexual infidelity: Evolutionary or logical inference explanation? *Current Psychology*, 20 (4), 327–336.

Frederik, D. A., & Fales, M. R. (2016). Upset over sexual versus emotional infidelity among gay, lesbian, bisexual and heterosexual adults. *Archive of Sexual Behavior*, 45, 175–191.

Geary, D. C., Rumsey, M., Bow-Thomas, C. C., & Hoard, M. K. (1995). Sexual jealousy as a facultative trait: Evidence from the pattern of sex differences in adults from China and the United States. *Ethology and Sociobiology*, 16, 355–383.

Sabini, J., & Green, M. C. (2004). Emotional responses to sexual and emotional infidelity: Constants and differences across genders, samples, and methods. *Personality and Social Psychology Bulletin*, 30 (11), 1375–1388.

Shackelford, T. K., LeBlanc, G. J., & Drass, E. (2000). Emotional reactions to infidelity. *Cognition and Emotion*, 14 (5), 643–659.

Urooj, A., & ul-Haque, A. (2015). Perception of emotional and sexual infidelity among married men and women. *Pakistan Journal of Psychological Research*, 30 (2), 421–439.

The Use of the Polygraph to Detect Lies of the Betraying Partner

5

Concerns about the Polygraph

I am troubled that the polygraph test is being used more frequently by couples trying to uncover the truth about infidelity, even as "the science" has not shown strong support for its effectiveness. Federal law no longer allows employers to use polygraphs, nor are polygraphs considered admissible as evidence in court. Yet many couples rely on them to either catch their betraying partner lying about some aspect of the affair or to demonstrate to the betrayed partner the truthfulness of their account of the affair.

Though the polygraph is called a lie detector test, it does not detect lies. It only detects changes in physiology. The polygrapher scores the test by comparing physiological responses (breathing, blood pressure, heart and perspiration rates) to these "probable-lie" control questions. The test results are not black and white as most people think.

Here is a basic description of how the test is scored: if the control response is larger than the relevant response, the score is ranked from +1 to +3, depending on the magnitude of the difference. If the relevant response is larger, the score is ranked from −1 to −3. The scores are summed over all repetitions of the questions asked to get to the total score. If the final score is sufficiently large and positive, then the subject is considered to have made truthful statements. If the final score is sufficiently large and negative, then the statements are considered deceptive. If the result is close to zero, then the test is inconclusive (Lewis and Cuppari, 2009).

It can be argued that the polygraph is more prone to seek out a lie than to seek out the truth, and it is even inherently biased against the truth. This is because the more honestly one answers the "control" questions, and as a consequence feels less stress when answering them, the more likely one is to fail (Maschke & Scalabrini, 2018) because of the greater distance between the control and relevant responses.

Alternately, people can beat the test by covertly augmenting their physiological reactions to the "control" questions. This can be done, for example, by thinking exciting thoughts, altering one's breathing pattern, or simply biting the side of their tongue. Truthful people can also use these techniques to protect themselves against the risk of a false positive outcome. Although polygraphers frequently claim they can detect such countermeasures, no polygrapher has ever demonstrated any ability to do so, and peer-reviewed research suggests that they can't (Maschke & Scalabrini, 2018).

Validity of the Polygraph

Although the polygraph is essentially the same for all applications, there are significant differences in the types of individuals who are tested, in the training of the examiner, the purpose of the test and the types of questions asked, among other factors. Therefore, saying that the test has any validity is difficult (Office of Technology Assessment, 1983). Significant review of the research literature has shown that there is little scientific evidence that the polygraph does anything close to detecting lies or the truth. Below are a number of quotes from the National Research Council (2003). The task of the committee was to review the scientific evidence for the accuracy of polygraphs.

- Almost a century of research in scientific psychology and physiology provides little basis for the expectation that a polygraph test could have extremely high accuracy.
- The theoretical rationale for the polygraph is quite weak, especially in terms of differential fear, arousal or other emotional states that are triggered in response to relevant or comparison questions.
- Estimates of polygraph accuracy from existing research overestimate accuracy in actual practice.

- Most polygraph testing procedures allow for uncontrolled variation in test administration that limit the level of accuracy that can be consistently achieved.
- The evidence (research) does not provide confidence that accuracy is stable across personality types, sociodemographic groups, psychological and medical conditions, examiner and examinee expectancies or ways of administering the test and selecting questions.
- Research on the polygraph has not accumulated knowledge or strengthened its scientific underpinnings in any significant manner.
- Further investments in improving polygraph technique and interpretation will bring only modest improvements in accuracy.

Polygraph advocates will argue that the decisive conclusions of the National Research Council were released over a decade ago and are not relevant, but contemporary research still supports the NRC initial conclusions. A recent research study reviewed the research since the landmark NRC findings and concluded that the quality of research on polygraphs has changed little in the years since the release of the NRC report, and that the report's conclusion that the polygraph has limited accuracy still stands (Iacono & Ben-Shakhar, 2019).

A Message for the Betraying Partner

At this point, I am assuming that you are working really hard to be truthful and to initiate offering information to your partner. Even with your best efforts, your partner may still be accusing you of lying. The frustrating aspect about telling the truth about the affair is that even after telling all of the truth, your partner may think there is more that you are not telling. You might even consider taking a polygraph so that you can show that you have told everything. As you might guess, I am advocating that you do not consider the polygraph test.

When You Are Accused of Continued Lying

We have discussed the different types of lies. Maybe, in fact, you are using one of these strategies and not recognizing it. Take time to consider if any of these types of lies are in play in your relationship right now. If so, commit to move away from these strategies and be more open with information to be more truthful.

As a reminder, there are lies by commission; these are the direct lies. The second type of lie is a lie of omission, which is a deliberate omission of information that alters the outcome. If you are withholding information to change your partner's judgement in some way, then it will appear that you are lying to him or her. The third type of lie is a lie of influence, which is meant to put the focus on the person lying and away from the truth, to make the liar seem like a good person.

Another concern about lying is being accused of lies when it is not true. The paradox could be that you did a lot of lying in the beginning when the affair was discovered, and now you are not. Now you are being truthful and still are being accused of lying. Let's look at a few different ways of managing accusations of lying (assuming that you are not!). From my experience working with couples, it seems that accusations of lies by commission, the direct lies, are a bit easier to manage.

The obvious first question to ask yourself when accused of lying is, "Am I lying?" You may have created a strong pattern of lying, and your immediate defensive strategy is to lie. If so, admit it, apologize, state the truth and let your partner know that you are committed to getting better with this.

Here is what I would suggest to do if your partner accuses you of direct lying:

First, stay calm. The way in which you respond communicates a considerable amount of information. Getting overly agitated or excited can actually make your partner believe the accusation is true.

Second, state your truth confidently. Begin by understanding that your partner is insecure in your relationship. Taking time to have empathy and validate this insecurity can be very helpful. Then state the truth and, if it makes sense, provide the evidence that you have. This could be showing emails or texts, or offering your phone for full viewing by your partner, or social contacts that can corroborate your truth.

Third, invite increased trust. State to your partner what you believe is the underlying fear or other emotion. For example, "I know that my affair deeply hurt you and you are worried I am going out after work and ... " Offer a suggestion on how you can be more trustworthy, or ask what you can do for your partner to regain trust.

Here are a few other recommendations that might be helpful. This is your "to not do" list.

Do not be indirect. Be direct in your responses and be precise. If you are not, it may give the impression that you are trying to go around the truth or making up something on the fly.

Do not repeat questions. Do not repeat the question being asked of you. This appears as a stall tactic and is actually used frequently by people who are lying.

Do not speak in the third person. Take ownership. Use phrases such as "I," "mine" and "myself." People who lie often remove themselves from the story by referencing themselves less when making deceptive statements (Van Swol et al., 2011).

For Reflection ...

If your partner tells you, "That's not true, you're lying," consider slowing the conversation down, take your time to respond thoughtfully, offer an expanded response from your perspective and ask how you can help them feel safe to trust you more.

Practice a lot of good will.
Be patient with your partner.
Broken trust takes time to heal.

A Message for the Betrayed Partner

You might want to ask your partner to take a polygraph. Just the decision alone can be highly stressful for the two of you and lead to conflict. A few couples have told me that taking the polygraph was helpful because it put the final questions to rest and allowed the betrayed partner to move to the next level of healing. Most couples, though, run into problems with the polygraph, and most tell me that the results did not lead them to a final answer about the truth. Here are some of the potential challenges with taking a polygraph test.

You will likely have the opportunity to plan the questions ahead of time. You may not be able to agree with your partner about the questions that will be asked. Depending on results during the test session, other questions may be asked by the interviewer that you may later disagree about their degree of usefulness or if they were even appropriate questions. Since you will not be in the testing session, you will have no control over how the questions are asked or have control of any follow-up questions.

Some of the questions may trigger a high level of emotional responses from your partner, which may make it difficult to discern if your partner's answers were emotional responses or actual lies. This could lead to false positives.

Here is a personal story from someone who went to a polygraph specialist to prove that he was faithful (DC585, 2019):

I have been with my girlfriend for almost 3 years and the first half of our relationship I was not totally loyal to her and had sex with a few of my ex-girlfriends.

I started going to a therapist to remove this destructive behavior from my life and then my girlfriend and I decided to go forward. Well I have done exactly what I said and stayed totally faithful to her and after a year, she did not believe me so asked me to take a polygraph test. I said sure and was actually excited because I figured it would prove to her I was telling the truth. Well, let's just say the examiner said I was lying to the question, "have you had sexual contact with anyone other than your girlfriend since Nov 14th 2015?"

I could not believe it and now I have both her and the examiner calling me a liar. I was telling the truth.

I assumed that I should retake the test with someone else and was aggressive in setting this up less than two weeks later. Well, guess what, I now have another examiner calling me a liar and he told my girlfriend he is 99% sure. So, basically, I am worse off now with 3 nails in my back and just confused by the whole process. Was I stressed about the question? Of course and I assume I did have a reaction to the question. I never should have destroyed her trust to start with and have been stressed about that every day since, but just because I had a strong reaction the question, the examiners are telling me I lied.

Ultimately, the majority of the couples that have shared their experiences with taking the polygraph have told me that they have mistrusted some or all of the results. Even when the outcome indicated no deception, the betrayed partner later began to think that the betraying partner has beat the polygraph because they were such a good liar. As the research shows, deception tactics are possible.

It is best just to avoid the polygraph altogether.

A Message for the Therapist

The polygraph was once considered a valid measure of detecting a lie. Modern research on the polygraph has demonstrated that the science behind it is weak, and it doesn't actually measure truth-telling or lying. As a result, polygraph results are rarely allowed in court anymore.

Today's polygraph is now recognized as being merely a measure of physiological arousal, which is only somewhat related to the truthfulness of a person. Physiological arousal, as measured by things like heart rate and sweatiness, are, in many people, evidence of feelings such as anxiety, guilt and shame. These feelings are sometimes related to deception, but more often are evidence of a person's feelings about the information or question.

Use of the polygraph in therapeutic treatment of infidelity and other sexual issues and behaviors is, at best, experimental without empirical support. Therapists using the polygraph as part of their practice and/or recommending the polygraph are suggesting a therapeutic treatment that has limited evidence of effectiveness and could cause harm.

The American Counseling Association (ACA) identifies that the counselor's responsibility is to use evidenced-based practices and techniques that do not harm, and I would extend this to therapists' responsibility to recommend only practices that are proven. The American Counseling Association states that when providing services, counselors use techniques, procedures or modalities that are grounded in theory and/or have an empirical or scientific foundation (ACA Standard C.7.a). In addition, the ACA states that counselors do not use techniques, procedures or modalities when substantial evidence suggests harm, even if such services are requested (AVA Standard C.7.C). Recommending the polygraph could be an ethical or legal violation, and you should weigh the decision carefully when deciding to use or recommend the polygraph as part of your practice.

Bibliography

DC585 (2019). Failed polygraph test on infidelity. Post to online message board. Retrieved from https://antipolygraph.org/cgi-bin/forums/YaBB.pl?num=1485365601, November 25, 2019.

Iacono, W. G., & Ben-Shakhar, G. (2019). Current status of forensic lie detection with the comparison question technique: An update of the 2003 National Academy of Sciences report on polygraph testing. *Law and Human Behavior*, 43 (1), 86–98.

Lewis, J. A., & Cuppari, M. (2009). The polygraph: The truth lies within. *Journal of Psychiatry and Law*, 37 (Spring), 85–92.

Maschke, G. W., & Scalabrini, G. S. (2018). *The lie behind the lie detector* (5th ed.). Published by AntiPolygraph.org.

National Research Council. (2003). *The polygraph and lie detection*. Washington, DC: Committee to Review the Scientific Evidence on the Polygraph Board on Behavioral, Cognitive, and Sensory Sciences and Committee on National Statistics Division of Behavioral and Social Sciences and Education.

Office of Technology Assessment (1983, November). *Scientific validity of polygraph testing: A research review and evaluation*. A Technical Memorandum. OTA-TM-H-15. Washington, DC: U.S. Congress.

Ratliff, B. (2011). *Behavioral cues associated with lies of omission and of commission: An experimental investigation*. Dissertations, 577. https://aquila.usm.edu/dissertations/577.

Van Swol, L., Braun, M., & Malhorta, D. (2011). Evidence for the Pinocchio effect: Linguistic differences between lies, deception by omissions, and truths. *Discourse Processes*, 49. doi:10.1080/0163853X.2011.633331.

6 Structured Disclosure

"Disclosure" is coming clean about the details of the infidelity. This is an early and vital step in infidelity recovery. Without disclosure, your chances of successfully rebuilding your relationship will be reduced.

Consider Kerri's reaction to my question "What did you most need after finding out about the affair?" (personal communication, February 12, 2018).

> On Discovery Day my world was thrown into chaos, I had no idea what was true or a lie in my life and my 30 years of marriage. What I believed was true, was now false. My life as I knew it was gone, erased, no longer existed. What I needed at that time was the truth and time with my husband face to face with no distractions along with a detailed, truthful timeline of their affair. How did the affair develop, how did they meet, what did they talk about, type of communications and how often (internet, Facebook, phone, letters, cards, what was it about her that he liked or loved so much, what type of places did they frequent when dining out, traveling? I needed good marriage counselor(s) and a personal therapy counselor to get through the trauma.

Here are characteristics of what I would consider disclosure for healthy affair recovery:

* The betraying partner makes the hidden world of the affair known to his or her partner as completely as expected by the betrayed partner.

- The disclosure includes facts about the affair relationship and places these facts in a developmental timeline of the affair relationship.
- The disclosure is initiated by the betraying partner.
- The disclosure is *shared* and *received* non-defensively.
- The disclosure includes sharing the internal experience of the betrayer, including thoughts, feelings, perceptions and expectations.

Failures in approaching disclosure in a healthy manner include interactions such as telling the truth only when there is insurmountable evidence to contradict either an untruth or undeniable evidence of hidden information, leaking out the truth over time, interrogations by the betrayed partner to get information, even accidental sharing.

Disclosure will be an emotional process for any couple. The more structured the process is, the less likely it will be that the discussion will devolve into a yelling match between the two of you. The goal, then, of structured disclosure is:

> for the betraying partner to willingly share accurate, expansive information about the affair relationship, sequentially, with questions and answers addressed without emotional intrusions and defensive responding from either partner.

Disclosure can be done privately between the two of you or facilitated by a therapist trained specifically in infidelity treatment. The decision should be guided by your assessment of your ability to stay emotionally regulated during the discussion. If this is a challenge for the two of you, I would recommend that you interview a few therapists and find a therapist who has done this before.

A Message for the Betraying Partner

Is your partner asking for more information? This could mean a number of things. Your partner could be struggling to make sense of the affair and just needs further explanation or clarification. It could also be that your partner is triggered by internal or external triggers, which results in questions for more information. It might be that you have lied in the past and your partner assumes that there must be more information that is currently unavailable to him or her.

Your partner's need for more information could also mean that you are withholding information or not being truthful. Only you know the definite answer to this question. Be honest with yourself. Are you withholding? Are you being untruthful?

You are about to make an important decision, whether or not to share information about your affair. An important consideration in resolving this decision is to identify what outcome you hope to achieve. Are you preparing for divorce and/or separation, or are you preparing to help heal the relationship for the two of you? Your answer indicates your next step.

If you are positioning yourself legally for divorce, which is a very protective position, it does not make much sense to disclose information to your partner about the affair. In preparing for divorce or separation, I would assume that you will need to be careful about what you say. A protective position will definitely not lead to successful recovery.

If you want to repair and strengthen this relationship, which is a vulnerable position, it will be critical for you to disclose what has been hidden. I recognize that if there is any threat of divorce or separation, it makes it more difficult for you to take the vulnerable position.

For Reflection ...
How might you work with your partner to remove the option of divorce or separation and help move you to a more vulnerable position?

Let me help you explore some other possible reasons why you might be withholding information of even lying. Perhaps you find it difficult to tell everything because you may be overwhelmed with remembering all the information about events, facts, thoughts, perceptions, details of who said what, time frames and the like. It might be helpful for you set down with pen and paper and answer all that for yourself.

It could be that you are withholding information for specific reasons that may or may not be within your awareness. Many people withhold information or lie about the truth of the affair when it is first discovered.

Maybe you too have decided to lie or keep parts of the affair hidden because you are not sure how to respond. It could be that you have chosen to lie so that you can stop the unraveling of the relationship or fear that sharing may end your relationship. Some people have told me that they lie because they are embarrassed or have extreme shame for what they have done. If any of these are characteristic of how you responded to the discovery of your affair, tell your partner that you have come to this awareness and are committed now to telling him or her information that you believe is important and that you are committed to answering all the questions that he or she may have.

Here are some other common reasons couples have told me in my clinical practice for not disclosing information about the affair. Consider if any of these are familiar to you.

- I do not know how to disclose information about the affair.
- My partner will know the true extent of my behavior.
- I am embarrassed. I am disgusted with what I have done.
- It is not in my nature to share deeply personal stuff.
- I am afraid of how my partner will react. My partner may become angry, escalate, attack the affair partner, show up at work.
- If my partner knows everything, he or she will never forget or will never be able to forgive.
- I am afraid of my own reaction. I will become depressed, make bad decisions, become suicidal, drink or use drugs.
- My partner will end the relationship. I will end the relationship.
- I do not want my partner to know that I am mourning the loss of the affair relationship.
- I am worried that if my partner knows more, he or she will disclose my affair to other family members, friends, coworkers or children.

Even though it is very common for people to lie when their affair is discovered, I am hoping that you will not do it. If you are doing it, I hope I can convince you to stop doing it immediately. To your partner, the past has been a lie, and the last thing they need is ongoing lies in the present.

Lies erode emotional safety, and without safety, trust and intimacy cannot be achieved. Your partner has a great sense of shock and loneliness now that he or she knows about your affair. The relationship that your partner shared with you is not what your partner thought it was. He or she now realizes that you had a hidden life that that they did not even know existed. What seemed real in the relationship with you can no longer be trusted.

> All statements are now judged by a new criterion,
> one that was not in use prior to the affair.

The deception of your affair has shocked your partner to the core. Your partner has lost a sense of identity. Feelings your partner experienced with you prior to the affair are now questioned for their legitimacy. One lesson learned from the deception is that your partner may not even be able to trust his or her own feelings. All statements are now judged by a new criterion, one that was not in use prior to the affair. Every feeling, statement and behavior must now be scrutinized for potential inaccuracies and judged based on your integrity and truthfulness. For now, your partner is on heightened alert, and this will continue until he or she feels emotionally safe. Remaining honest for your partner will help them begin to trust their own intuition again and spend less energy on assessing what is true and what is not.

Deception, Leakage and Lying: Is There a Difference?

If we can agree that any form of deception is a lie, one form of deception is leaking out truth over time. One couple that I worked with called this "trickle truth"; I refer to it as leakage. Nothing around my house works well when it is leaking. Leaking "truths" do not work well, either. This strategy causes extreme distress because it causes a resurfacing of thoughts and feelings similar to when your partner first learned of the infidelity. It is as if they have returned to that awful day when they discovered your affair.

Let me take a moment to compare two possible hurts for your partner. One is leaking out information over time, and the other is sharing the hidden truth of your affair. Sharing the details of your affair will be painful for your partner to hear, and certainly something you are trying to avoid, but my argument would be that it will be a short-term hurt for your partner that is necessary for him or her to make sense of things.

However, withholding the truth and leaking out bits of information over time can create lasting hurt that could haunt your relationship for years to come. The leaking perpetuates your partner's ability to discern what is true and what is not. It also supports your partner's belief that you lack integrity and cannot be trusted. From your partner's perspective, lying by omission is still lying, and it is judged in the same way. This is more difficult to overcome through the long haul. It is better to get the whole truth out all at once.

When infidelity is discovered, it is as if the events of the past demand that they be viewed from a new perspective. Many aspects of the relationship will now be examined from a new lens. Your partner will wonder what were you really doing when you left early from your child's birthday party two years ago, who you were really talking to on the phone so much during your last vacation or who were you really meeting for lunch. *Left in ambiguity, your relationship will linger in suffering and not heal.* It is worse to leave it to your partner's imagination than it is to tell your partner the truth. Current research suggests that leaving it to your partner's imagination will cause significantly more emotional pain than if you just told the truth (Pazhoohi et al., 2019).

It took considerable energy for you to conceal the affair relationship. It also takes considerable energy to conceal the truth. This energy could be put to better use. The depth of involvement in the affair relationship and the context has to be known to your partner. These insights need to be incorporated into each of your understandings of the affair relationship before any stability or significant change can occur in the relationship.

For Reflection …
Will you take the risk to be vulnerable, embarrassed, angry, frightened and more, to open this world up to your partner so that he or she can heal?

Bringing Truth to Light

When the hidden world is brought to light, an accurate view of the affair relationship and your primary relationship can appear. This will be important because after your relationship stabilizes, you will need to uncover the drivers of the infidelity, whether it resides within yourself, problems in the relationship, external stressors placed on the relationship or past history that is getting in the way of intimacy in your primary relationship. This cannot be done by the two of you if only one of you has the information to completely assess the situation.

Should I Share Everything?

Now, let's take a moment to consider what to share. In the counseling profession, there is some debate about this. Some counselors will tell you that you need to disclose most or all of the details of the affair. Others will recommend that you should be careful to limit sharing details about the sexual experience with the affair partner, so that you are not creating, for your partner, strong imagery of sexual encounters with the affair partner. The reasoning is that these imageries may be difficult for your partner to forget. From my perspective, I would suggest that you give as much detail about all aspects of the affair as is required from your partner. He or she will let you know how much they want to know.

Telling a high level of detail about your affair may actually increase the odds that you will save your relationship. Peggy Vaughan, in her book *Help for Therapist and Their Clients* proposed that 86% of married couples who discussed the infidelity "a lot" stayed married (and living together) versus 55% of those who discussed the infidelity "very little." So, concerning disclosure of your affair, more is better.

I have also found that when one partner does not disclose the information about the affair to the other, this nondisclosure has the potential to increase your partner's drive to discover the truth. Your partner may begin investigating the affair, which can include gaining access to computer and email communication, searching phone transactions to discover unidentified phone numbers, contacting the affair partner, contacting the affair partner's spouse and interviewing people at work, church or school who may know information or may be withholding information. Investigating has the potential to escalate out of control.

> A betrayed partner investigates from a place of pain
> that grows as their investigation continues.

A professional investigator approaches their work from an unbiased position; a betrayed partner investigates from a place of pain that grows as their investigation continues. For couples attempting to recover from an affair, investigating behavior by the betrayed partner will steal the energy needed to stabilize the crisis and repair the relationship. If the goal is to stay together, disclosure is important. Disclosure should happen early, and the information should be offered willingly.

Consider the following story, which recounts Danielle's experience of her husband's unwillingness to disclose, her experience of investigating following discovery of her husband's affair and the impact on her final decision to divorce (Danielle, personal communication, January 1, 2018).

> On a fall afternoon, as my kids were napping and I was making casseroles to freeze, a man came to my house and told me his wife and my husband (co-workers) were having an affair. It was traumatic, but I was so glad this man came to tell me. I had been suspicious of my husband for four years prior with another co-worker, and flat out asked him if he was having an affair. He told me no. I trusted him.
>
> But after the man came to my house that fall afternoon, I took matters into my own hands. I became the investigator. I could not trust my husband. I had to investigate others on my own. I spent the next week tracking down a select few co-workers and former girlfriends, and even the husband of the woman I was suspicious of from four years prior.
>
> My husband has always been private; now I realized "secretive" would be a better word to describe him. My investigations gave me the power in the relationship. I felt stronger, more informed because of my own "research." Instead of trusting my husband and relying on him to be forthright (which he wasn't doing), I absolutely needed to do my own investigations. My husband remained tight-lipped during this time, barely disclosing any information.
>
> I discovered a lot about my husband. He had a pattern of preying on younger, vulnerable women at work. I discovered this by my own inquiries. It was empowering to me to do my own investigations. It was absolutely helpful to me. We are getting divorced.

My husband was unwilling to be forthright and honest. He has always been private (secretive), but in a time like this when honesty is most important, he was unwilling to open up. If a marriage is going to survive infidelity, opening up is essential.

For Reflection …

What kind of partner do you want to be during this stressful time in your relationship?

What is keeping you from telling the whole truth?

How will your disclosure increase trust and stability in your relationship?

What is the impact of your deception for your partner?

How will not giving an expansive response to questions fuel investigating in your partner?

What will be found out if your partner investigates? What will be the consequence of this discovery? Would you rather he or she find out from you or someone else?

Please take the time now to consider how you are approaching disclosure about your affair and if you are interested in changing your approach. The preceding questions can help you create some specific insights about your decision around disclosure or nondisclosure, the reasons behind the decision and its potential impact.

Disclosing your affair in the form of a developing story makes the most sense.

Structuring Your Disclosure

So how do you go about disclosing information to your partner? I suggest that you use a structured approach that is planned by the two of you before you begin the process. Disclosing your affair in the form of a developing story makes the most sense because your partner will hear how the affair began, how it developed and how it ended. Adding in the context (where you were, who was there, what you did, thought and felt) and answering questions for your partner – as you tell the story – will add to the completeness of the story.

Preparation for Disclosure

Begin your disclosure by confirming with your partner that you want to share everything you can about the affair. Remember that every person is different in what they want to know and what they want to share. So, it will be up to the two of you to negotiate the decision about what will be discussed.

To help in this process, I have created a template of potential content areas that might be useful. Share the template outlined in Table 6.1 with your partner and ask if there are any questions that he or she would include or exclude from the template. The template covers considerable information, and it is likely that your partner will not want all of it included. Also, your partner may want specific information related to your affair that is not included in the template. Once your partner has responded, set a time when the two of you can be alone and talk.

Before you sit down with your partner to tell the story of the affair, get organized. Bullet-point content to discuss in each of the categories (Beginning of the Relationship, Development of the Relationship, Ending of the Relationship). List items you are going to discuss, and also try to predict what questions your partner will have and include these in your topics. This process will be very difficult for you to do. It will also be very difficult for your partner to hear.

When it's time to share the information, reaffirm your commitment to share completely. Both of you can reaffirm that you will create non-defensive communication and work hard to care for each other's emotional needs. You should share first without interruption by your partner. Your partner will write out any questions that come to mind and ask them after you have completed sections of the disclosure template.

Go purposefully slow and allow time for your partner to think about what they are hearing from you. If you notice that he or she is writing, stop for your partner's thoughts and questions to develop.

Table 6.1 Template for Disclosure of the Affair Relationship

Section 1: Beginning of the Relationship

- Discuss exactly when you first met. Tell how you connected and if anyone helped get the two of you together.
- Discuss what attracted you to this person.
- Discuss what was going on with you at the time.
- Discuss if there were other affair partners that may be discovered.

Section 2: Development of the Relationship

- Discuss what were your regular places to meet, such as restaurants, hotels, parks.
- Discuss what technology you used to meet the affair partner or to communicate (Signal, Kik). Identify any subscriptions you have (AdultFriendFinder, Ashley Madison).
- Discuss who were supporters of the affair. These would be people who actively kept your affair hidden or knew the affair was occurring and didn't say anything.
- Discuss if there were accidental meetings with friends and family members while with the affair partner. Did friends and family figure out what was going on?
- Disclose if the affair partner has your cell phone number or any additional personal information (place of employment, home address, etc.).
- Disclose what gift-giving occurred and identify the gifts. Identify how they were purchased. Identify what mementos of the relationship you saved, such as cards, letters, emails or pictures. Identify where these mementos are now, and what you plan to do with them.
- Discuss if you gave the affair partner money or purchased any major purchases for the affair partner (car, house).
- Identify other "discoverables," information that you have failed to share and now want to share in good faith to help your partner's recovery.

(continued)

Table 6.1 (Continued)

Section 3: Emotional and Sexual Aspects of the Relationship
• Identify the feelings you had for the affair partner; for example, did you fall in love with the person?
• Share what you told the affair partner about your primary relationship and if you discussed the problems in your relationship. Share if you ever felt guilty, and if so, did it change your behavior?
• Identify what the affair partner felt for you and if there is still a possibility that the affair partner still has feelings.
• Discuss when the relationship became sexual and in what circumstances.
• If your partner is interested, discuss the sexual behavior of the relationship. This may include sexual behavior such as intercourse, oral, anal or other behaviors.
• Discuss if you or the affair partner used a condom every time during sex. Discuss the context of when you had unprotected sex.
• Identify where and when you met for sex and if sex occurred in your home, at work, in a car, hotels, a park or other public places. Disclose all locations.
• Discuss when you met for sex with the affair partner – day of week, time of day.
• Discuss if you took off work or met for sex when your partner was out of town.
• Discuss how often you had sex.
• Discuss if you used drugs or alcohol during sexual encounters.
• Disclose if it is possible that a pregnancy could result from one of your sexual encounters.
• Disclose if photos or videos were taken by you or the affair partner during any sexual encounters. Discuss sexting and virtual sexual encounters. Does any of this remain?
• Discuss what role pornography had in your affair behavior.

Section 4: Ending of the Relationship

- Discuss who ended the relationship, and how it ended.
- Identify what expectations the two of you set at the end of the affair relationship.
- Identify if you thought about contacting the affair partner to say goodbye.
- Discuss if you have contacted the affair partner after the relationship ended or if the affair partner tried to contact you. Explain what you plan to do if the affair partner attempts to contact you.
- Discuss how you feel about the affair partner now that the relationship has ended. Do you miss the person? Discuss if there are times when you still want to be with the person.
- Identify if the affair partner is in a committed relationship, and if so, discuss if their partner knows about the affair. If so, discuss how this was disclosed.
- Discuss if you have been tested for STDs and the outcome of the test.

Section 5: Healing the Primary Relationship

- Discuss what you feel for your partner today. Discuss love, appreciation, guilt/shame, hurt, remorse or other feelings.
- Describe what you plan to do to demonstrate that you are 100% into healing this relationship. Consider those things that have been requested by your partner.
- Identify what you will do to prove that you are worthy of trust from your partner. Specifically describe your daily trust behaviors.

Here are the steps in the structured disclosure process:

1. Each partner will read this chapter completely.
2. Each partner will review the template. The betrayed partner will edit the template and submit an edited version to the betraying partner, who will have made additions and deletions to the template.
3. The betraying partner will get organized and prepare to answer all items on the template.
4. The betraying partner will share the items sequentially as the betrayed partner only listens, writing down comments and questions to ask at the end of each of the five sections in the template.
5. At the end of each section of the template, the betrayed partner will ask intentional, quality questions, and the betraying partner will answer expansively.

There is one key consideration I want you to consider when answering questions for your partner. Be careful with your use of the phrases such as "I don't know" or "I can't remember," because it will be difficult for your partner to accept. Your partner may interpret your response as evasive or lying. Certainly, there will be times when you will not know or can't remember. Yet, you can still address the question without actually knowing the specific facts that your partner is requesting. I would suggest not using these phrases at all, since there is always an answer to any question that your partner may ask. Even when you don't know the specifics, you can still answer the question.

A good way to answer any of your partner's questions is to answer the question as expansively as you can. Answer questions using any of the following categories:

1. Your behaviors.
2. Your thoughts.
3. Your feelings.
4. Your perceptions of yourself or others.
5. Your expectations of yourself or others.
6. Place any of these in the past, present or future.

Each category can be discussed from the perspective of the past, the present or the future. In other words, you could answer how you felt about the affair partner when the two of you first met or what your perception of the affair partner is now. As an example, even if you don't know the actual day that you met with the affair partner for your first sexual encounter, you could answer that you met after work and went to a hotel for several hours (behaviors); that you considered not going to the hotel but ignored your better judgment (thoughts); before going to the hotel you felt excited, but you felt guilt after going (feelings); and you believed that what you did would never be forgiven by your partner (perception).

Hearing the truth can be very painful for your partner, even though your partner needs the truth to move through the healing process. At times, your partner may respond with extreme hurt or anger, and you may want to stop because of your partner's responses. At these times, it can be helpful to resist responding defensively and to validate your partner's perspective. Defensive responses can be interpreted by your partner as that you just don't understand their pain or that your partner is not worth the effort.

Validation is simply responding to your partner by restating his or her perspective and stating that your partner's (feeling, perspective, expectation) are valid from their perspective. For example, "You are hurt that I took him to our favorite restaurant. I agree that it damages the memories that we created at Rio's and you may never want to go back." When things get hot in the conversation, respond with empathy and validation.

One last thing I would like to mention: Your willingness to disclose will make a huge difference. When you willingly disclose difficult information, it provides hope of more disclosure in the future, and hope that the relationship can be mended.

Pain Is Inevitable

Sharing about your affair will be bring up pain for your partner. The risk is that the pain will feel so great to your partner that he or she will consider stopping the process or, worse, ending the relationship. If your partner expresses that the pain is great, slow down the process and focus on just listening to your partner, not being defensiveness, and empathizing and validating when you can. The focus should be on just listening without trying to fix anything. Your compassion can be a very healing experience for your partner.

A Message for the Betrayed Partner

Since the two of you are reading this book, this may be the first time that both of you have a clear understanding of why to disclose and a structured method for getting the information that you need about the affair. With that said, how do you go about *obtaining* and effectively *hearing* the information about the affair? Certainly, how you go about asking the question will make a difference in the quality of information you obtain. Also, how you go about hearing the information is just as important, because how you react as you seek information can generate more information or restrict disclosure. How you hear the information can also make sure that the information is retained and processed properly. The task at hand is to get accurate and complete information so that you can create an informed understanding of the affair in context to your relationship. You can do this through the structured disclosure I am proposing here.

My hope is that after reading the first section of this chapter, your partner will begin to willingly share information about the affair in a non-defensive way. I'm hoping that the two of you will discuss the contents of the disclosure template and negotiate what information you believe is important for you to have. I would expect that the two of you would get together and systematically work through the information on the template. Sometime this is useful to do on your own, but sometimes couples want to do this with the help of a therapist. Usually, the decision rests on how confident the couple is about sharing the information without escalating.

My expectation is that your partner will initiate disclosure and be expansive in his or her answers. I also recognize, though, that there are things that you can do to increase the success of disclosure and meeting the goal of obtaining accurate and complete information, so that you can establish an informed understanding of the affair in context to your relationship.

I also have expectations for you. Primarily, I suggest that you try to stay calm. Yes, that is easy for me to say and difficult for you to do. I recognize that hearing the information can be highly emotional to hear. But if you escalate or interrupt your partner's sharing, you limit your ability to get the information.

When your partner is sharing the information from the template, I would recommend that you only listen, and when questions or thoughts arise, write them down. You can ask these questions or share these thoughts once your partner has completed each section of the template.

Emotional Regulation

Your emotional regulation is important to this process. If you are emotionally volatile, your partner is unlikely to disclose. Emotional regulation means that you have the ability to shape the emotions you have, when you will have that emotion and how you want to express it. Emotional regulation means that you have control over your total emotional experience.

Certainly, it is important for your partner to know how you feel. However, when you are trying to obtain and hear information about the affair, you are better served by monitoring and managing closely your emotional experience. It might be best to share your feelings at another time so that you can get the information that you need.

Another interaction during disclosure that it is not helpful is to aggressively attack the answers that you are receiving. Again, challenging attacks may reduce your partner's interest in continuing to share. As you hear the truth of the infidelity, it is likely to bring out even more deceptions. As you are working through the disclosure process, I would recommend that you try to appreciate the current truthfulness than to attack the past deceptions.

Let's consider the art of questioning. All questions have purpose, but too often people ask questions without considering the intent of the question. For example, is the question meant to influence you or your partner? For the purpose of this structured disclosure, you will ask questions to only influence you. For that reason, you will ask questions that will get information and do no responding. You will not share what you think and feel in this process.

> Our emotions can be an informing component of decision-making, but when they are overwhelming, they blind our objectivity.

Pain Is Inevitable

I want to state a brief and obvious statement: Pain is inevitable in this process. Know that the truth is going to hurt. The risk is that the pain will feel so great that you are unwilling to continue. Some couples will begin the disclosure process, decide the pain is too much and end the relationship. I would suggest that you do not make important decisions while going through this process. Our emotions can be an informing component of decision-making, but when they are overwhelming, they blind our objectivity.

Factual Questions

Questions that begin with what, when, who and where tend to be factual in nature and are useful in creating your understanding of the events, timeline, locations and people involved. When asking factual questions, it is important that you keep your own opinions out of the conversation so that you can get a clear record of the events.

How and why questions need a little more forethought because if you are not careful, they can lead to defensive positioning by your partner. How questions, if used to question your partner's character or integrity, may interrupt your process of disclosure. "How could you?" is a question that comes to mind.

Why questions are strategic questions that assume that the person being questioned is in the wrong. For example, asking your partner "Why did you do that?" assumes that they should not have done it, resulting in your partner defending the position. Avoid why questions and be careful with how questions.

Ask questions for clarification or expansion; save challenges for a later discussion. Try to keep you and your partner non-defensive. By the way, defensiveness is a hallmark of the beginning stages of escalation. It will be important for the two of you to guard against defensiveness.

There are a number of common ways that I see couples creating defensiveness during disclosure. Defensiveness will increase if your partner:

- Does not demonstrate a willingness to answer questions or share.
- Refuses to answer specific questions.

- Appears evasive.
- Omits critical information.

Remember that there are also ways that you might create defensiveness during a structured disclosure, derailing your efforts for complete disclosure. These are:

- Attacking the character of your partner.
- Calling the affair partner names, usually evoking some kind of defending of the affair partner.
- Aggressively challenging your partner's answers instead of asking more quality questions.
- Not managing your emotional experience.

A Message for the Therapist

Therapists have strong opinions about the importance or appropriateness of the betraying partner sharing the details about the affair. Some therapists will suggest that details should be kept to a minimum. They think that details, especially sexual specifics, will cause too much hurt or create intrusive images that will be difficult to forget. Couples, though, tell a very different story. From my own practice experience, most, but not all, betrayed partners insist on knowing everything about the affair from start to finish. Peggy Vaughan (2002) completed an interesting survey of 1,083 married spouses hurt by infidelity, and her data clearly showed that getting answers to questions and thoroughly discussing the details of the affair increase both the likelihood of maintaining and rebuilding the marriage and increase the likelihood of recovering from a spouse's affair. For example, when couples were asked, "Did you want to know details about the affair?" 93% of the group wanted information, while 62% said they wanted to know everything about the affair, including details. Only 7% said that they did not want to know. There are very few gender differences, by the way, in these findings; in fact, men and women were within only a few percentage points of difference in need to know the details, both wanting a high level of disclosure. This need to know is driven by the betrayed partner's attempt to make sense of what happened.

Most people who had an affair are reluctant to disclose information. The common attitude regarding disclosing details of the affair is that once the partner is caught, they will say as little as possible. In Vaughan's (2002) survey, almost half of those individuals participating in affairs told the details of the affair only after much pressure to do so, and another 28% refused to share any details beyond the mere basics. Individuals that I have worked with offer explanations that indicate that they are protecting their partner from further harm, which falls short with their partner and oftentimes me. In truth, not disclosing is usually causing more harm, not protecting from harm.

An important aspect in recovering from any traumatic event involves telling the story about what occurred (Glass, 2015). From the betrayed partner's perspective, it is critical in most instances to work for obtaining as much detail about the affair as feels comfortable for them. It is warranted for the therapist to work not for complete disclosure, but for the amount of disclosure that is required from the betrayed partner.

Another aspect of this disclosure is the willingness of the betraying partner to disclose these details. Vaughan (2002) believes that the "willingness to disclose" has a positive impact on recovery and sustaining the marriage because it provides hope for greater honesty in the future. However, failure in "willingness to disclose" is interpreted by the partner as hiding essential information about the affair.

As the work toward disclosure begins, it is beneficial also to discuss the importance of disclosure in the recovery process as mentioned in the previous discussion. The betrayed partner should be directed to be careful not to lie or even "lie by omission," because when the omissions are discovered, they are perceived by the betrayed partner as continuing to be secretive, untrustworthy and unwilling to share, and this results in perceived setbacks in healing for the betrayed partner.

Another disclosure that is useful for the betrayed partner answers the question "How were you able to do this?" Considerable efforts were made to keep the affair hidden, and until the betraying partner was caught or they disclosed, they were able to deceive their spouse to a large extent. The betrayed partner may want to ask questions around what the participating partner did to create this deception.

When One Partner Argues against Disclosure

I have heard this on occasion: "I am not going to tell anything about the affair. You do not need to know anything. It will not be helpful." Usually, when I explain the clinical reasons for disclosure as stated earlier, the person will modify their position and begin some form of the disclosure process.

When I have a person who steadfastly argues against disclosure, I gently help the partner to reflect deeply on their core values and discern if the refusal to disclose is in alignment with those values. I do this through Socratic questioning and exploration through three lenses – legal, ethical, and moral perspectives. The following is a short guide of a discussion that I follow that offers potential questions and thoughts that you could direct to your couple from each of these lenses. This discussion might go something like this:

Legal Lens

When I discuss the legal perspective, I am talking about all the expectations that the two of you identified as you defined and developed your relationship. These include concerns such as exclusivity, trust, commitment to the well-being of the relationship and the partner, career, faith, children and the like. I call this the original agreement. These are the legal aspects of the relationship. Most couples are also quite clear on what is illegal for their relationship.

I want to take a deeper look into this original agreement and flesh out the assumptions that you have about not disclosing. For example, what was the original agreement that you made in forming your relationship or getting married? What were some of the explicit and implicit understandings of what it means to be a couple? What were your expectations around interacting with "attractive others"? What did you decide about allowing for relationships outside this relationship? What were the expectations about keeping secrets from each other? Did the agreement allow for hiding important information from each other that may affect the health and vitality of the relationship or to make an accurate assessment of the relationship?

Ethical Lens

An ethical relationship is characterized by both partners consistently demonstrating honesty, loyalty, openness, integrity, respect, fairness and accurate communication. How are these demonstrated in nondisclosure? Also, two primary ethical constructs are beneficence, which means to do good, and nonmaleficence, which means to do no harm. Considering nondisclosure, are your behaviors ethical in the sense that they demonstrate that you are interested in doing good and not doing harm?

Moral Lens

What is your own understanding of what is right and wrong? What does it mean to you to be a good person? Is this in alignment with choosing not to disclose about the affair? Here are a few virtues of a couple coming from a strong moral position:

1. The partners show compassion by trying to understand the pain of their partner and wanting to do something about it.
2. The partners show cooperation by helping each other in times of need.
3. The partners show courage by having a willingness to do difficult things when it is for the benefit of the partner or the relationship
4. The partners show fairness, by acting in a just way even if it is uncomfortable.

Preparing the Couple for Disclosure

Facilitated disclosure is an anxiety-producing experience for the couple and the therapist. There are a number of things that I would encourage you to do to help the couple predict the experience of disclosure and to reduce anxiety. One of the primary ways you can reduce stress for the couple is to make sure the couple has trust that you are in charge of the process. They will need to know that you have a clear plan, that you have done this before, that you are confident and competent in facilitating the process and that that you have had success.

Couples need to be aware that affect regulation is critical and that you have a high expectation that they will monitor this during the process.

When the betrayed partner remains calm, increasing disclosure by the betraying partner can occur. You will need to help the betrayed partner understand that it is to their advantage to stay calm. To assist with affect regulation, set expectations to take breaks and stay alert for flooding by either partner.

Just like structured enactments, everything that is going to occur in the process should be told up front to the couple. There should be no surprises. I discuss two possible ways to manage disclosure and ask the couple which alternative best fits them.

Self-Guided Disclosure

I assign the betraying partner the task of reading this chapter and completing the disclosure template in preparation for disclosing the information to the betrayed partner. Once complete, the couple schedules time together in a quiet, private environment to have this discussion. The betraying partner will then share the information with the betrayed partner. The betrayed partner will listen quietly, take notes and try not to interrupt. The betrayed partner can ask questions following each of the five sections after the information is shared. The betraying partner will work to be non-defensive and expansive in answering. Many couples choose this option because they do not want to wait until the next therapy session. The experience is then processed in the next session.

Therapist-Facilitated Disclosure

My preferred method is to assign the betraying partner the task of completing the disclosure template as a between-session task and then share the information with the betrayed partner in session. Both partners would read this chapter, the betrayed partner would edit the template and give it to the betraying partner, and the betraying partner would complete the template in preparation for disclosure in the next session.

Therapist-facilitated disclosure will allow you to ensure emotional safety, interrupt problematic communication, keep the focus on revealing the content of the disclosure template and encourage the expression of feelings. Couples choose this option when they believe that they will have difficulty managing emotions.

The Use of Disclosure for the Therapist

Knowing the details of the affair is also helpful to the therapist for treatment planning. It helps you understand the challenges ahead in treatment, helps you tailor the treatment to the couple, identifies early boundaries that might need to be set to support recovery, and help uncover potential referrals that might need to be generated. Fife, Weeks, and Gambescia (2008) recommend several content areas that will be useful for the therapist in initial treatment planning considerations, including:

- The type of infidelity (whether emotional, sexual, etc.).
- The level of deception that occurred.
- The time frame or duration in which the infidelity occurred, the frequency of communication and/or sexual contact and the location of encounters.
- History of past infidelity (might include previous affairs and/or sexual addiction).
- Relationship of the affair partner to both partners (friend, coworker, neighbor).
- Degree of collusion by the betrayed partner.
- Perceived attractiveness of the affair partner.
- Social and cultural context of the infidelity.

Bibliography

Fife, S. T., Weeks, G. R., & Gambescia, N. (2008). Treating infidelity: An integrative approach. *The Family Journal: Counseling and Therapy for Couples and Families*, 16(4), 316–323.

Glass, S. (2015). Reflections by Glass: The trauma of infidelity. Retrieved January 16, 2015, from http://www.shirleyglass.com/reflect_infidelity.htm

Pazhoohi, F., Silva, C., Pereira, L., Oliveira, M., Santana, P., Rodrigues, R., & Arantes, J. (2019). Is imagination of the infidelity more painful than actual infidelity? *Current Psychology*, 8, 572–578.

Vaughan, P., & Vaughan, J. (1999). *Recovery from affairs: A handbook for couples* (p. 6). La Jolla, CA: Dialog Press.

Vaughan, P. (2002). *Help for therapists (and their clients) in dealing with affairs*. LaJolla, CA: Dialog Press.

7 **Rebuilding Trust**

A Message for the Betraying Partner

This chapter is mostly for you. You have betrayed the trust in the relationship, and therefore the responsibility for repairing the trust falls on you. I know that you need trust from your partner as well, and I will encourage your partner to maintain trust as you repair your relationship. However, the repairing of the broken trust is on you.

Regaining trust will take hard work on your part. This hard work, though, is required of you if you plan to keep this relationship. It may seem like a surmountable, and maybe unfair, task at the moment as you watch your partner struggle with asking multiple questions, investigating for evidence and experiencing rapid emotional dysregulation. Your partner may even be telling you that they will never trust you again. Maybe, but I would not trust that statement if both of you are willing to make the necessary effort to repair the relationship. I have seen many couples in this same circumstance, and they have been able to regain trust.

Consider the complexity of trust. Trust is a function of the characteristics of the person and has contextual and temporal variables. Most common definitions of trust focus only on the person. The Oxford dictionary defines trust as a firm belief in the reliability, truth or ability of someone (Oxford Online Dictionaries, 2017). Merriam-Webster (2017) defines trust as the assured reliance on the character, ability, strength or truth of someone. These dictionary definitions are incomplete because you need to consider the contextual and temporal factors.

Table 7.1 Trust Equation

Character Strength + Context Changes + Time = Increased Trust in the Relationship

Self-reflection on your own personal characteristics will be beneficial for you in assessing how you might strengthen your own character. As you assess this, I will help you learn important behaviors within these character domains that will help your partner trust you more.

Trust is contextual; your partner may trust you in one context but not the other. For example, your partner may trust you while you are at work, but not when you go to lunch with coworkers. As you develop trust in the different context of your life, trust is created even if your partner does not completely view you as a trusting person.

In this regard, you grow into being a more trusting partner by (1) strengthening your character, (2) focusing behavioral changes in specific context and (3) maintaining these efforts consistently over time. To make the concept simpler, look at the equation in Table 7.1. This is what I call the trust equation, and it will help you increase trust in your relationship.

In the rest of this chapter, I will discuss ten characteristics of a trusting partner. This is the "character strength" of the first part of the trust equation. I will describe each characteristic and then identify the behaviors related to that characteristic that are specific to the recovery of infidelity. I will ask you to consider behaviors for specific context and encourage consistency over time.

Characteristics of a Trusting Partner

Integrity

Integrity is about having strong principles. It is doing the right thing, consistently, even when no one is watching. As you strengthen your integrity, try living from a more virtuous perspective. In risky situations, instead of asking "How should I behave?" ask "What kind of person should I be?" Integrity is embedded in your character, and you should behave consistently with truth, honesty and compassion, regardless of what others think or do. Demonstrate integrity by:

- Start to think of yourself as someone that your partner should and can trust. Thinking of yourself this way is the first step toward making it happen. Live your values and principles in all settings with all people.
- Think of the values that you want to demonstrate to your partner. Directly state them to your partner.
- Tell your partner directly that you want them to trust you again.

Honesty

Honesty is a complex concept. It is more than "not telling a lie." In its basic form, honesty is *speaking* and *acting* the truth. To be honest, you will need to *speak* the truth with your partner in a respectful and empathetic way, intending to increase your partner's personal understanding and even increasing your partner's personal growth. *Acting* honestly also implies your willingness to include fairness in dealing with your partner and the refusal to engage in deceit or secrets. Demonstrate honesty by doing the following:

- Stop lying immediately. After betraying your partner's trust, you will only hurt your partner more by continuing to lie, changing variations of the truth, hiding information or denying aspects of the truth. Do not protect your partner's feelings by hiding parts of the truth – you really are not protecting him or her, you are creating more harm.
- Today, tell your partner that you want him or her to know all the details of the affair. Provide the complete story up front, and do so voluntarily. When questions are asked, answer them completely.
- Make sure all future statements are truthful.
- Bring all secrets to light so that they can be understood.

Reliability

To be reliable, your partner will need to believe that you can be depended on consistently for your character, judgment and behavior. When you commit to doing something, your partner can depend on you to keep that commitment. If you can be trusted to be reliable with the little things, you will be trusted with the bigger things. Start small and think big. Demonstrate reliability by doing the following:

- Evaluate your commitments on a daily basis. Identify which commitments are a high priority. Commitments that you make to your partner should be a high priority.
- Do not overestimate your ability to keep a commitment. Keep in mind the time needed for the commitment and the other commitments that will be competing for this time.
- Do not always say yes. Do not commit to anything that you cannot follow through with. If you believe that you can't make a commitment, be honest and say so. When your partner can trust your "no," they will also be able to trust your "yes."

Accountability

To demonstrate accountability in your relationship, openly share how you spend your time and energy throughout the day. Share where you have been, where they intend to be, who and what gets or does not get your attention.

Your partner will trust you more when you take responsibility for your contribution to the relationship, for good and for bad. You should act in good faith for the relationship, and when in error, you accept that error, report it to your partner and explain the situation. Demonstrate accountability by doing the following:

- Each day, tell your partner your plans for the day and who you will be with. At the end of the day, review the same. Yes, it may feel like you are seeking permission or that your partner is keeping tabs on you. Remember, you kept a part of your world hidden from your partner, and what seemed to be reality was not. Any secret now will damage the trust you are trying to build.
- If you have erred in some way, disclose it and discuss it with your partner.

Advocacy

To advocate for the relationship means to care and nurture the relationship. Pay special attention to the state of the relationship and have sensitivity to when things go awry. Quickly attend to repairing when tension occurs in the relationship or conflict arises. Demonstrate advocacy by doing the following:

- Today, ask your partner if he or she is eating, sleeping, etc., and whether he or she is doing okay. This may seem basic, but if your partner is in a traumatic state, he or she may not be functioning normally and may be too distraught to convey this to you or even meet his or her own personal needs.
- Help find something for your partner to enjoy and encourage your partner to participate in these activities regularly.
- Daily, notice either the early warning signs or behavior signs that your partner is triggered and implement the intervention(s). Your goal is to limit or eliminate your partner's triggers. Triggers are a challenging experience for your partner and can lead to significant damage over time. Triggers are external or internal cues that lead to distress. External triggers could be any sight, sound, smell, location, date of the year, a scene in a movie or television show. Internal triggers can include passing thoughts, intrusive or reoccurring thoughts, physical sensations, feelings toward you (positive or negative), defensive reactions from you or comments from other people. You can help your partner with the emotional and behavioral experiences when triggered. When your partner becomes dysregulated and escalates, take time to listen and calm the experience. Notice when your partner is quiet and offer to talk.
- Next, sit together and identify three common triggers that he or she is experiencing.
- Talk about what behavioral signs you see associated with these triggers. This will help your respond with compassion when you see them.
- Ask for specific things to do when he or she is triggered (interventions).

Vulnerability

It is in risking greater vulnerability in a safe relationship that one can grow in trust and become more intimate. This occurs in part because emotional exposure by both partners and a willingness to be curious and understand will create greater intimacy in the relationship. At the deepest level, directly exposing your pain to each other and receiving a compassionate response will help heal the emotional wounds of the affair. Demonstrate vulnerability by doing the following:

- Seek out your partner's pain and find opportunities where you can compassionately respond.
- Stay calm when your partner is not, and focus on validating and empathizing.
- Stay curious about your partner's perspective and try to really understand the perspective, particularly when the perspective is different from yours.
- Today, initiate one conversation with your partner about some aspect of the pain you caused with your affair. Listen with compassion, without defensiveness, and show curiosity by asking questions. Try to get a deeper understanding of what he or she is going through. Your interest will show to your partner that you have not forgotten the pain you caused and that you are a partner in his or her healing.

Accessibility

Pragmatically, to be an accessible partner, you will want to answer the phone when your partner calls or respond to voicemail and text in a reasonable time. At a more intimate level, consider being accessible by sharing your internal world to your partner, without the need for any prompting on their part. Being accessible means sharing your thoughts, feelings, convictions, longings, fears and doubts. Demonstrate accessibility by doing the following:

- The more open you are about what you are doing, the less urgency your partner will feel to check in on your activities. Ease his or her insecurities by letting your partner know what you are doing and checking in with messages or quick phone calls when you are not at home.
- Remember that your phone, email, voicemail and social media account were all in commission of your affair. More than likely, they may feel like sources of secrets and lies to your partner. If you choose

to provide voluntary access to these things, your partner may trust you more quickly. You are sending a message that you have nothing to hide. If you cannot offer this access, it would be fair to question what you are indeed hiding.

- Today, invite your partner to go someplace that you typically would go alone. For example, invite him or her to go out with you and your friends or to work out together.

Presence

Intimate, trusting relationships take effort, and both partners need to have a strong personal presence in the relationship. To be personally present means that you will need to commit a great deal of energy to being mentally, physically and emotionally available to your partner. Spending time together is a priority, and the time together should be intellectually and emotionally engaging. In times of crisis, you should make your partner a priority over everything else. Demonstrate personal presence by doing the following:

- Your partner needs opportunity to work through things with you, so you need to be spending plenty of time together. You will need to be emotionally available and, equally as important, your physical presence will help your partner feel valued.
- If you can't be with your partner physically, keep your phone with you whenever possible so that that your partner has access to you. They may not even need to call or text you, but knowing where you are available may help them see you as making an effort to be available to them in multiple ways. Send text messages of love and share that you are thinking about him or her throughout the day.

Transparency

To be transparent is to make intentional choices to allow important information about the relationship health and fidelity to easily and consistently be available to your partner without requiring a direct request for the information. Nothing in your communications to anyone outside of your relationship should need to be so private that it could not be shared openly and willingly with your partner. Demonstrate transparency by doing the following:

- Just because your partner does not bring up the infidelity does not mean it is not on your partner's mind. It probably is on his or her mind much of the day. When you are thinking about it, let your partner know. It gives the message that you are still aware of the pain that you have caused and that you have not forgotten and moved on.
- Avoid saying "I don't know," "I can't remember" or "It just happened." Instead, respond with expanded descriptions of how you behaved, what you thought at the time or how you felt at the time. Any one of these responses is better than "I don't know."
- Don't forget that you are also hurting, and maybe you feel that you do not have the right to share your feelings. When you are sad, share it. Just make sure that you do not state it in a way that discounts your partner's feelings. For example, don't say "I am feeling sad too." That would be discounting.

Commitment

Commitment is the mutually agreed-upon promise that you made to be exclusive. It means that you are "closed" to other emotional and physical relationships. To demonstrate commitment to your partner, create a barrier to all others that might pose a risk to the rebuilding of the relationship. This barrier protects the intimacy of the relationship and helps you to be dedicated to the growth, health, passion and vitality of the relationship.

- Your commitment in the relationship is damaged and fragile. It is important that what you say and do conveys a new level of commitment.
- If you have not already done so, end the affair openly and immediately. There should be no undercover meetings with the affair partner to say goodbye. Any message or contact with the affair partner should be in full view of your partner.
- Be patient with the healing and recovery process; it shows your commitment to the relationship.

- Make your partner a priority again. Definitely show your appreciation that they are willing to stay in the relationship with you.
- Show your partner love, go to new places, try new activities. In essence, you are creating a new relationship with him or her.

Context Changes

Context changes are the second part of the trust equation. Ask your partner to help you identify what they need to feel emotionally and physically safe in your relationship. Use Table 7.2 to have your spouse identify from the list those actions that will make an immediate impact for increasing trust. It might be helpful to just circle the items (or part of the items) that would be most helpful directly on the page. After the items have been selected, suggest to your partner to identify the three actions that would be a priority, knowing that more can be selected later. If you believe that you can give your 100% commitment to the actions that your partner identifies, then agree to do them. If you do not believe you can be committed to the actions, do not agree to do them. Remember, the trust characteristic of "reliability" requires that your partner can depend on the commitment. Once you have committed to the actions, do them with vigor and consistency.

Take time now to ask your partner to identify the context in which he or she trusts you the least. Below are just a few ideas just to get you thinking about possible context that might need focused work. Once the context is identified, find out what behaviors will help make you more trustworthy in that context.

At work/after work	With friends	At a bar/restaurant
On trips	On the computer	With extended family
With a specific person	Late at night	When drinking alcohol

Time

Time is the last part of the trust equation. Begin each day with a commitment to being consistent in your moral character and behaviors. Consistency is the key element of time. Since a trusting relationship requires consistency over time, the feeling of trust may not occur for quite a while,

Table 7.2 Trust-Building Actions

Concerning You ...	Concerning Me ...	Concerning Others ...
Tell me how you feel; share your intimate thoughts and feelings with me.	Call or text me during the day.	Send communication to the affair partner telling them the affair is over and you want no contact.
Let me know how you think and feel we're each doing getting over the hurt.	Recognize that I am anxious and not yet trusting, and reassure me.	Tell me when you inadvertently see or connect with the affair partner.
Tell me what you need from me.	Answer all my questions about the affair, without defensiveness, even when they are asked multiple times.	Tell me when you have been contacted by the affair partner.
Share with me what upsets you during the day.	Share your positive feelings about me.	Tell me if you are planning on contacting the affair partner.
Tell me what pleased you during the day and what you are proud of.	Share your negative feelings with me in an open, non-defensive or attacking way.	Come home from work and have dinner with the family.
Tell me when you feel I've let you down or hurt your feelings.	Plan time to be alone with me.	Quit hanging with friends who are a bad influence.
Work on letting your anger go and getting back on track with me.	Spend time connecting with me and work on rebuilding our verbal, physical and sexual intimacy with words, actions and questions.	Get a different job.
Be aware of and understand your old patterns in our relationship and stop yourself from returning to them.	Listen to my positive and negative feelings, and don't try to "fix" things; listen, be curious and ask if I want suggestions or help.	Make your cell phone, bank statements, credit card statements and email accounts available to me. Keep no private accounts.

(Continued)

Table 7.2 (Continued)

Concerning You ...	Concerning Me ...	Concerning Others ...
Understand your longings in our relationship so that you are aware of your blind spots. Express this to me.	Focus on what I'm saying and don't be distracted when we talk.	Move to another city with me.
Understand and accept that your affair will come up throughout our lives and understand that this is normal and not done to retaliate.	Show me affection outside the bedroom.	Attend couples therapy with me. Answer all of my questions in front of the therapist and explore the reasons for your infidelity.
Resist the temptation to push me to heal faster.	Be romantic with me.	Limit your overnight travel.
Give up drugs, alcohol, porn or other unhealthy behaviors. Replace with exercise, good diet and recreation.	Hold me and show understanding when I'm upset; don't give up on me.	Come home on time, call me when you will be late, don't stay out late.
	Point out to me in an open way my old patterns and when you believe I am slipping back into these.	Don't go out with friends at night. Do not eat lunch with coworkers who I am insecure with.
	Tell me when you are tempted to reconnect with the affair partner.	Take time off work and spend the majority of your time with me.
	Tell me all the places you met the affair partner for sex, romantic getaways or other meetings.	

even when you are demonstrating trustworthy behaviors. This requires a good dose of patience.

Actions Speak Louder than Words

I want to state this again because I hear it over and over again in therapy. Actions speak louder than words. This is the reason for the extensive list of behaviors in Table 7.2. Consistent trust-building actions over time make the difference.

Trust-Eroding Behaviors

Is it possible that as you are trying to develop trust, you are also doing trust-eroding behaviors, potentially without even knowing it? Take a moment to reflect on what you are potentially doing to erode the trust in the relationship. Confirm this with your partner. A discussion on this topic might also be helpful.

> *For Reflection ...*
> Actions speak louder than words. Take time now to write down a list of trust-promises that you have made to your partner. Have you been meeting these promises? How do you assess your performance? Consider linking actions to these promises and assess these actions daily.

A Message for the Betrayed Partner

I am putting most of the responsibility for rebuilding trust in your relationship on your partner. He or she is the one who chose to have an affair, and so it is proper that your partner is the one who should rebuild your trust. I make this point because your partner chose to resolve their personal or your relationship problems by having an affair, so they are responsible for recreating trust. The two of you will need to resolve the relational issues, but for now, your partner needs to demonstrate to you that they are worthy of your trust.

With that said, it may be difficult for your partner to trust you. He or she may have great fear that you will end the relationship or that you will publicly share information to hurt them. Your partner may share similar insecurities related to emotional vulnerability, sexuality or your relationship with others in your world. Ask your partner what they most need to feel more secure in your relationship and consider using that as a guide to maintain the trust that they had with you prior to the affair. Also, consider implementing items from the chart that you might do to help your partner.

A Message for the Therapist

Ultimately, trust in relationships is a multidimensional construct that when in place results in a trusting relationship. Therefore, trust is the fruit of a trusting relationship. *Each partner has to have the primary characteristics of trustworthiness and intentionally contribute these characteristics to the relationship through thought and behavior in a variety of contexts, consistently over time.*

The Temporal Aspect of Trust

When couples talk in session about re-establishing trust, they most certainly recognize that it will take substantial time and intentional work. It can be helpful to discuss trust in terms of mechanisms of temporal change and how this affects the re-establishment of trust. According to Vanneste, Puranam, and Kretschmer (2014), there are several ways in which time effects trust, including initial bias correction, change through contextual experience and trust-based selection and identification.

Initial Bias Correction

Before entering any relationship, a person may be pessimistic, optimistic or unbiased in their perspective about the other person's trustworthiness. This orientation comes from past experience in relationships and family of origin. A pessimistic person underestimates trustworthiness, an optimistic person overestimates trustworthiness and an unbiased person makes an accurate estimation. As the relationship develops, the person gradually moves within the relationship to a more accurate assessment of trustworthiness. This initial bias has an effect on both the willingness to begin the relationship and the evolution of trust within the relationship once it is established. For a person who has an unbiased perspective, trust will remain constant over time.

For couples trying to recover trust, their early formation of trust in the relationship may give a clue to how long the recovery of trust will take. It would make sense that a partner with a pessimistic perspective at the start of the relationship may take a longer period of time to re-establish trust.

Change through Contextual Experience

Understanding context can be clinically useful. First, trust-building efforts can and may need to be directed at specific context, such as demonstrating boundaries when out with coworkers. Second, couples can rebuild trust in specific context even when overall trust is either low or high. For example, trust building can take place in a specific context, even when the trust in the relationship is vulnerable. This allows for general and targeted interventions. You can help couples identify the contexts that need to be strengthen and develop specific goals for increasing trust in those contexts.

Trust-Based Selection and Identification

Recovering trust is hard work. Over time, unsuccessful experiences in relationships play a crucial role in the evolution of trust. People prefer to maintain relationships with trustworthy partners. The good news is that consistency in trust-reinforcing behaviors can lead to the decision to stay in the relationship, but the bad news is that trust-eroding behaviors will lead someone to leave the relationship and to prefer not to be with someone with similar characteristics. Your role is to help the couple to identify and understand the role of trust-reinforcing and trust-eroding action.

Trust as a Function of the Characteristics of the Person

Trust is more than a combination of behaviors. Trustworthiness also is a function of the characteristics of the person. When someone harms trust in the relationship, it is these characteristics that have been breached for the person who had the affair. Many individuals will say that their affair was not in their character and that the affair violated their own values. They are speaking to these specific characteristics.

Bibliography

Merriam-Webster (2017). *Definition of trust*. Retrieved March 10, 2017, from https://www.merriam-webster.com/dictionary/trust.

Oxford Online Dictionaries (2017). *Definition of trust in English*. Retrieved March 10, 2017, from https://en.oxforddictionaries.com/definition/trust.

Vanneste, B. S., Puranam, P., & Kretschmer, T. (2014). Trust over time in exchange relationships: Meta-analysis and theory. *Strategic Management Journal*, 35, 1891–1902.

8 Managing Intrusive Thoughts and Images

"Will these thoughts and images ever go away?" This is a common question that I get, and for the person experiencing intrusive thoughts, the answer is that it is hard to imagine that they will. Recovery from infidelity can be long and slow, but with time and compassionate work between the two of you, the intrusive thoughts and images will be less intense and less frequent.

I want to take a moment to tell a story that often is credited to the Native Americans (Lenape or Cherokee) but more likely from Christian evangelist Billy Graham (1978, p. 92). The story was meant to drive home the concept of the battle between good and evil, and I want to borrow the story to frame another battle that some people experience. Here is how I tell the story to couples that I work with:

> A Native American grandfather and grandson are sitting together and the grandfather shares, "I had a dream last night that there was a fight going on inside me. It was a terrible fight between two wolves. One was aggressive, fearful, resentful and concerned mostly for itself. The other had patience, humility, empathy, generosity, and compassion. These wolves were fighting to the death." The grandfather and grandson sat quietly for a while taking in the quiet space of the story. "Which wolf won?" the boy asks. The grandfather simply replies, "The one you feed."

A similar conflict is played out internally for someone hurt by infidelity. Intrusive thoughts may be running rampant in your head with little relief. The thoughts are distressing and include intense emotions of anger, fear and sadness. They occupy the space that once included patience, empathy and compassion for self. Which do you feed?

Along with intrusive thinking, couples also talk about experiencing intrusive images, so I make that distinction here. Intrusive thoughts are highly emotional and involve an intense reliving of the event in the present. Most are likely to last for a period of minutes and can be accompanied by physical sensations. Distressful images may also accompany the intrusive thoughts. It is common for people to have one to four highly repetitive trauma images, mainly of short duration (Reynolds & Brewin, 1999) and they are not necessarily related to the infidelity itself.

Here is the task before you. These intrusive thoughts and images are dysregulating to the relationship, and it will slow down and hamper recovery. So, it is important that both of you know to what extent each of you are experiencing intrusive thoughts and images and work to reduce them immediately.

A Message for the Betraying Partner

You can feel fairly helpless when your partner becomes upset because they are responding to thoughts and images that they are experiencing. One minute you are cuddling on the couch, and ten minutes later, your partner is angry and lashing out at you. You find yourself asking, "Where did that come from?" It seems like such a drastic shift in mood. You then respond out of frustration because it feels like such a setback.

How in the hell can you manage that, right? How long will these episodes continue before they stop? Will they ever stop? Can you do anything to help?

I would start by saying that there are certainly things that you can do to make things worse, yes, I said worse, because I want to emphasize that you can contribute to the problem, and you can contribute to the solution. Not contributing to the problem is also part of the solution. So, let's start there, what you should not be doing.

Not Knowing Your Partner's Internal Experience

Do you know how much your partner thinks about your affair? If you are similar to many of the couples that I work with, you will be shocked at just how many times your partner (a) has transient thoughts and correspond-ing images about your affair and (b) full episodes of rumination which can last a considerably long time. I believe that if you know the extent of these two types of disruptive thoughts, you will have a clearer picture of the pain your partner is in. The impact of knowing, I hope, is that you will spend more time knowing your partner's pain and sitting with them when they are in pain, comforting, so that they do not feel alone in their healing.

Later in this chapter, I will ask your partner to "catalog" his or her intrusive thoughts and images on a shared document on Google Drive. I want you to take this activity seriously and *initiate* reading and discuss-ing the document each evening with your partner. Notice themes in your partner's writing and discuss them with your partner. Offer compassion and validation as you discuss the writing. Be curious about the meaning your partner has about the thoughts. Encourage your partner to ask ques-tions about your affair. I have found that this activity alone helps reduce intrusive thinking and rumination.

Not Bringing the Affair Up to Talk about It

There is a common scenario that couples tell me about that occurs in many different contexts. The couple is out to dinner, and someone walks by who resembles the affair partner. Both partners see this person and recognize the similarity. The betraying partner thinks, "Shit, that person looks just like_____. I don't want to bring it up, it will be too upsetting and ruin the evening." The betrayed partner thinks, "How could [the betraying partner] do this to me? I am so stupid to not have known, how embarrassing." Both partners sit in silent pain. As you are now aware, what starts out as a passing thought in your partner's mind may develop into rumination on the thought until your partner explodes in an aggressive manner, seemingly too late to do anything about it.

Next time a scenario like this happens, whether it is at home watching television, at the movies, in the mall or at a work or social event, privately and quietly make a simple statement that goes something like this: "I am thinking about what I did and maybe you are too." It acknowledges that you are aware of the potential thought-trigger and offers an invitation to talk. It may also cut off an episode of ruminating for your partner that will end in a hurtful exchange between the two of you.

Saying "I Know How You Feel"

Saying "I know how you feel" in no way demonstrates that you know how your partner feels and may even feel very hollow to your partner. This is a common way to say, "I am connecting with your hurt," but in truth, most people who have affairs know little about what it feels like to be cheated on. Since we never really know the complex experience of how someone feels, it is better to stick with empathy responding, such as "You are hurt because I did this." In other words, the structure "You feel because ____" tells your partner that you have heard their emotional expressions. The structure of simple empathy responses is mainly to indicate a feeling and then indicate a reason for the feeling. Here are a few examples:

You feel <u>devastated</u> because <u>Jenny was your best friend</u>.
You feel <u>betrayed</u> because <u>you always perceived me as devoted</u>.
You feel <u>afraid</u> because <u>our future is uncertain now</u>.

> For Reflection …
> Consider five feelings that your partner is experiencing and write down an empathy statement for each feeling. Make sure the statement identifies the feeling and the reason for the feeling. Invite your partner to listen to these statements and notice your partner's reaction to each statement. Ask your partner to respond to each.

Offering False Assurances

You have probably caught yourself saying similar statements like, "I will never do this again, trust me," "It will get better" or "I wasn't near that part of town today, so you do not need to be concerned."

Discounting your partner's perception is tricky because you want your partner to have the facts straight. "You must have loved her," "I will never be able to trust you again," "I will never get over this" are statements that can be frustrating and hard to hear. It is how your partner is feeling in this moment. As you continue to help your partner heal, these statements will diminish in strength and frequency. It is better to validate the underlying meaning and state how you might help in healing. For the examples I just mentioned, validating statements of underlying meaning could be: "It's hard for you to imagine that I didn't love her and I intend to help you understand that relationship completely," "It will take a lot of work on my part to help you trust me again and I want you to know that I am willing to do it" and "It's hard for you to see an end to this pain, and I want you to know that I am open to talking anytime about anything."

Sharing Your Guilt and Shame

Your partner is working on the pain that you caused. It is very possible that when you share your shame and guilt, it could lead to emotional flooding of your partner. It would be wise to be very selective in timing when to bring up this topic, and definitely not when your partner is emotionally flooded or triggered. I am not saying that your feelings should not be talked about, but you will need to be very careful not to make any discussion diverted to your shame or more about your shame than your partner's pain when your partner is dysregulated or confrontational.

Responding Defensively

You will need to be careful not to respond defensively. If you regularly respond with defensiveness when you are questioned about details of the affair, the message your partner may receive is that they are not worth the work. Certainly, you can't let your partner abuse. The best bet is to help your partner manage the hurt and pain by being a good, compassionate listener or take a break if discussions become abusive.

A Message for the Betrayed Partner

Couples have told me that they have upwards of 50–100 thoughts or more a day about the affair. These are the intrusive thoughts that light up like fireflies on a summer night. The light flashes with a memory, a fear, a hurt; and many stay only momentarily and then go away. One person that I worked with personified her thoughts, saying "some are fleeting and some dwell for hours," suggesting that the thoughts do as they wish and are not a part of her own process. She called the experience emotional roulette. As a therapist, I know that the dwelling for hours was truly in her own process. Dwelling is ruminating; it is obsessive thinking. As you may have experienced, obsessive thinking is a process that moves like a river to a sea of emotional distress. You have ownership in this process. You need to stop the freight train of rumination.

I wish that I could offer you a quick, maybe even magical, solution to relieve you of the thoughts and images that haunt you. These quick strategies don't exist. What I will suggest in what follows are a few strategies that you can do on your own to interrupt rumination. I also have one strategy that I would like you to do with your partner, and I will start with that one.

Cataloging

Your partner is likely not aware of how much intrusive thinking and how many distressful images that you are experiencing. This activity will open up a window to your internal world so that your partner can get a clearer picture of how much distress you are truly in. My hope is that by knowing this, it will compel your partner to work hard to help you reduce the intrusive thoughts and images.

Start by making a shared document on Google Drive. As you go through your day and you experience unwanted thoughts or images, catalog them on the Google Drive document. Once cataloged, move on from the thoughts to some other activity. This is an important part of the process, so make sure to do it. Continue doing this throughout the day. If at some point you have the same thought or image, catalog it again because it will help your partner know the themes in your experience and the persistence of the thoughts and images. Again, move on to another activity once you have cataloged the thought.

I have asked your partner to review this document at the end of each evening and initiate a discussion with you about what they have read. Help your partner understand what meaning you make about the thoughts. Express your feelings calmly and help your partner understand what you need based on your discussions about the images. Many couples tell me that this is a useful activity in reducing the frequency and intensity of the unwanted thoughts. One betrayed partner stated the benefits of this activity for her were (Losey, 2017):

- Not feeling so isolated with their thoughts.
- Helped reduce her own curiosity about facts and events.
- Gave her permission to ask multiple questions and to ask the same question more than once.
- Allowed her to write the questions down and filter out the thoughts that were just angry questions.

Refocusing from the Internal World to the External Experience

Obsessive thinking is an internal process. Maintaining the internal process allows for rumination and disengagement from real-world experiences. It will be helpful for you to get out of their head and to be more engaged in the real world around you. Mindfully focusing on a behavior can be beneficial. Refocusing on what is happening now in the moment, or even taking the time to practice mindfulness, can be useful.

Shifting to a Predetermined Thought

In this strategy you will need to shift from the negative, obsessive thought to a more reasonable alternative thought. Rather than attempting to "stop" the obsessive process, it works by shifting your attention to a predetermined thought. For example, you could state, "These are just thoughts, and they are not helpful" or "I am okay, and I will now refocus on my work."

Practicing Distraction

Many couples find success by simply distracting the thought by doing some alternative activity, even if it is for only ten minutes. The simpler, the better here; activities such as going for a brisk walk, playing with your child or pet or playing a video game can help disengage from the obsessive process.

Intrusions in the Sexual Experience

Though not as common, some couples will say that they experience intrusive images during sex with their partner. This can be a rattling experience that can stop you from being sexual. To avoid this becoming a barrier to your ongoing sexual relationship, it might be helpful for the two of you to try to manage the intrusive image as it occurs.

First, allow the image to be there. Let it have its mental space, and do not attempt to block it or alter it. Blocking strategies tend to increase the intensity and frequency of the image.

If it feels right to you, share with your partner that you are experiencing the image or thought. If your partner responds with empathy (which is what I am asking your partner to do), the empathy might be enough to help you move right back into the sexual experience.

Next, focus on the sensual experience. Intentionally focus on the body-to-body sensations with your partner, taking in the experience with all your senses. Take turns touching each other, starting with your partner touching you and you only concentrating on what it is like for you to be touched. Only talk if something is uncomfortable. After a few minutes, take time touching your partner, and concentrate on what it is like to touch your partner. This is a process called sensate focus. In a later chapter on erotic recovery, I discuss sensate focus in greater detail. Doing sensate focus as a means to manage the intrusive image may move you uninterruptedly back into the sexual experience. Later or even the next day, discuss the image with your partner and what it means to you.

A Message for the Therapist

Couples (and therapists) seem unprepared for managing this problem and will ask for concrete strategies to reduce or eliminate the obsessive thoughts. Desperate to help the couple, the therapist introduces cognitive strategies that have worked for other anxiety and depressive disorders. Therapists need to be aware that many of the cognitive behavioral therapy techniques that they use for other anxiety issues may actually worsen symptoms of intrusive thinking.

Though it may seem logical to work with the person to stop the thoughts or force the thoughts out of their mind, my guess is that "thought stopping" rarely works. In fact, research suggests that attempts to stop obsessive thoughts may only intensify obsessive thinking (Hubbard, 2015). Even worse, some therapist will use the "snap the rubber band on the wrist" technique or simply saying "stop" to oneself. These too will lead to worsening of the symptoms.

Wait a second – why is thought-stopping ineffective? There are a number of things occurring for the individual that are powerful perpetuators to the obsessive thinking. Out of obsessive thinking grows several rituals, including thinking a "good" or "safe" thought, or seeking self-reassurance. Often the goal of reassurance is to obtain 100% certainty as to whether the obsessive thought is accurate. Individuals report that they would feel relief even if they were to determine that the obsessive thought was accurate, because at least they would then be certain about how to proceed (Purdon, 2004). However, when a person tries to suppress a thought, there is actually a rebound effect in which the previously unwanted thoughts are present more frequently, and at a higher intensity.

Imaginal Exposure

I believe Exposure and Response Prevention (ERP), a treatment protocol for Obsessive Compulsive Disorder, will help individuals in managing obsessive and intrusive thinking. One primary intervention from ERP that I will discuss here is imaginal exposure (Foa, Yadin, & Lichner, 2012) and how it can be applied specifically to the treatment of intrusive thinking and unwanted images in infidelity treatment.

Imaginal exposure involves asking the person to imagine in detail the distressing thoughts or image. It is used primarily to help confront the consequences that the person fears will occur (their partner will cheat again, their partner is continuing to hide evidence) if they do not perform a behavior (investigating emails, reading blog posts incessantly or other behaviors the betrayed partner may do).

It can be helpful to explain to the couple the reasoning behind asking the betrayed partner, and sometimes the betraying partner, to imagine such a distressing experience that they have been trying to avoid up to this point. I explain that imagining the distressful thought in detail several times may help them have the thought without experiencing high levels of anxiety. This is the prime reason for the intervention. They will also be able to accept their negative thoughts and feelings by coping with them, instead of trying to get rid of them or avoiding them. Lastly, the person will learn that having negative thoughts will not make them happen (Foa, Yadin, & Lichner, 2012).

A simple way this exposure can be accomplished is to ask the partner to write out the thought or scene in vivid detail. Time should be given to this so that the partner is writing more than just a sentence or two. The image should be written out as if it is happening in the moment. You may want to do this part in session with the partner. Once it is written, ask the partner to read it out loud several times, each time assessing their level of anxiety.

Image Re-Scripting

Imaginal exposure can be combined with image re-scripting to take the power from distressing thoughts or images. Image re-scripting is a therapeutic technique that can be used to address specific memories associated with the disclosure or discovery of the infidelity. It can be a very powerful therapeutic intervention when the therapist can assist the client in changing the memory's course of events to a more desired direction. This can be done in session and then utilized consistently out of session.

Therapists use re-scripting differently. For some therapists, the re-scripting is carefully prepared with the partner before imagined, usually by creating awareness of the dysfunctional appraisals of the image or memory. The re-scripting is then implemented directly, with the therapist instructing the partner to imagine the prepared new script. In other approaches, the partner tries re-scripting on the basis of wishes he or she experiences while imagining the memory; and in still other approaches, the therapist develops the script altogether (Arntz, 2012).

I typically work collaboratively with the couple in re-scripting. In session, we will identify the image or scenario that is distressful. The individual is instructed to imagine the negative memory or image as vividly as possible, as if it were really happening in the here and now. Following the image, we work together to identify the elements of the memory that needs to be changed to a more positive direction. I will then ask the partner to write out the positively directional script in great detail. Once the script is written, I will ask the partner to read it out loud. The partner is instructed to do two tasks post-session:

1. Make a recording of the script on their phone and play it multiple times per day.
2. When the negative memory occurs, experience the memory but develop it in the direction of the positive script.

For an example, let me briefly describe a situation with a young couple named Jenn and Abe who came to me due to Jenn's infidelity. Abe was having reoccurring images of descending the stairs of his home to find the affair partner downstairs ready to kill him. This image was highly vivid for Abe, and this led to a pretty lengthy negative narrative. For this image, we were able to change the characters, the setting and the time that the event occurred, all leading to a better outcome. He then used the written script of the transformed scenario to record on his iPhone to listen to repeatedly.

Bibliography

Arntz, A. (2012). Imagery rescripting as a therapeutic technique: Review of clinical trials, basic studies, and research agenda. *Journal of Experimental Psychopathology*, 3(2), 189–208.

Foa, E. B., Yadin, E., & Lichner, T. K. (2012). *Exposure and response (ritual) prevention for Obsessive-Compulsive Disorder: Therapist guide* (2nd ed.). New York: Oxford University Press.

Graham, B. (1978). *The holy spirit: Activating God's power in your life*. New York: Warner Books.

Hubbard, B. (2015). Obsessive thinking, worry and cognitive-behavior therapy. Retrieved July 30, 2015, from http://cognitive-behavior-therapy.com/cognitive-behavior-therapy-forobsessive-thinking-worry-rumination/.

Losey, B. (2017). *Creating an effective couples therapy practice*. New York: Routledge.

Purdon, C. (2004). Cognitive-behavioral treatment of repugnant obsessions. *Journal of Clinical Psychology*, 60(11), 1169–1180.

Reynolds, M., & Brewin, C.R. (1999). Intrusive memories in depression and post-traumatic stress disorder. *Behaviour Research and Therapy*, 37(3), 201–215. doi:10.1016/s0005-7967(98)00132-6.

9 Managing Triggering Experiences

A trigger in its basic form is simply a signal of some sort that leads to a dramatic change in behavior, mood or thinking. In relationship to infidelity, this signal takes the person back to the vulnerable, "danger" state when he or she learned about or discovered the affair. These signals can come from internal or external experiences. External signals could be any sight, sound, smell, location, an anniversary date or a scene in a movie or television show. Internal signals can include passing thoughts, intrusive or reoccurring thoughts, intrusive images, physical sensations or feelings about your partner.

Triggering is part of the trauma experience of infidelity. One of the most important concepts to understand is what happens when a triggering experience occurs. There is a transition from a "calm state" to a "state of emergency." Sometimes I will refer to this as a dysregulated state. There can be dramatic changes from a sense of calm to a perceived state of emergency. This can really affect a variety of areas of functioning, including feelings, thoughts and behaviors, and even disrupt the person's sense of self. The overall goal is to help the person who is triggered to maintain calm and stay regulated – and to stay engaged with their partner.

A Message for the Betraying Partner

Your affair is now imprinted on your partner's brain. The imprint will fade over time, but it is forever there. I know that if you could, you would love to go back into the past and change your decisions and your behaviors.

As the saying goes, you truly are unable to change the past. But I can tell you now, you have considerable control and ability to change the impact of the past.

> You have the power to help
> your partner heal,
> to heal faster,
> and to managing the distressful, triggering moments
> that will be frequent immediately following your affair.

You have the power to help your partner heal, to heal faster, and to managing the distressful, triggering moments that will be frequent immediately following your affair. You also have the power to cause further hurt and damage to the relationship by doing nothing, or worse, by being frustrated, dismissive, defensive or demanding when your partner expresses hurt, mistrust or confusion.

I am sure that by now you have experienced your partner being triggered, by observing your partner experience a triggering event, or maybe you have tried to help in some way. Take a moment to consider triggering experiences for your partner. What triggers your partner? Is it internal or external? Is it a scene on a television show? How you dress? Driving by a specific location? How do you behave, talk or express something when your partner is triggered?

One of the primary ways to help your partner regulate his or her emotional experience is by creating a social environment of support. The social environment, of course, is you and your relationship with your partner. Your relationship can be a healing place for infidelity recovery; in fact, it is the best place for recovery, even better than therapy.

When your partner starts to emotionally dysregulate, your healing response of offering calm, caring, nurturing and empathy will help your partner stay in control and stay engaged with you. The connection that you have with your partner that continues through the troubling triggering experience helps heal your partner. Think of the opposite – your partner disengages from you. What do you suppose they are thinking when they are disengaged? Really, take a moment to consider what they are thinking. I have a strong suspicion it is not positive.

So, the goal is to help your partner stay regulated and to stay connected with you. It is important when one partner is escalating that the other partner stay rationally detached. This means that your role in the escalation matters. To be rationally detached, you will need to manage your own behavior and attitudes and not take on the emotions of your partner. One way to do that is through what I call compassionate responding. Here are a few important features of compassionate responding.

Compassionate Responding

Sometimes your partner's triggering experience will include asking you questions or telling you the hurt they are experiencing. Begin by allowing yourself to hear your partner's message without judgment. In doing so, you can more effectively take your partner's perspective and help him or her process the many difficult emotions they are probably experiencing.

I liken it to momentarily putting the spotlight on your partner and only managing what your partner is experiencing. You are helping your partner experience you in a compassionate way, without your integrating your own "stuff" into the conversation.

We briefly discussed responding with empathy in a previous chapter. Now let's look at it in more detail. It is better to *demonstrate* that you understand than it is to *say* you understand. So, resist the temptation to say, "I understand," and demonstrate that you understand both the *feeling* and the *meaning* of what your partner is telling you. Later, you can integrate your ideas about the situation. Consider our examples from the last chapter. Each of these demonstrate understanding of feeling and meaning as underlined in the following.

You feel <u>devastated</u> because <u>Jenny was your best friend</u>.
You feel <u>betrayed</u> because <u>you always perceived me as devoted</u>.
You feel <u>afraid</u> because <u>our future is uncertain now</u>.

You can take these statements to a deeper level by adding in validation. Two ways to validate are to "validate in principle" or to "validate in fact." To validate in principle with one of these examples, you might say "You feel betrayed because you always perceived me as devoted. Our devotion to each other was critical in our trust." Validation in fact would sound something like this. "You are feeling hurt because I lied to you. You are correct, I did lie. I should not have done that, and I am sad that I did that."

Now let's revisit our examples and include either "validation in fact" or "validation in principle." Can you recognize the type of validation used in our examples below?

You feel <u>devastated</u> because <u>Jenny was your best friend</u>. *My actions risked the loss of our relationship and ended your relationship with Jenny.*

You feel <u>betrayed</u> because <u>you always perceived me as devoted</u>. *Our devotion to each other was always critical in our trust.*

You feel <u>afraid</u> because <u>our future is uncertain now</u>. *It is important for me to understand how my actions make you fearful.*

You can still take the empathy response to an even deeper level. By adding in goal direction, you convey an intimate level of understanding. Starter phrases can be used to signify goal direction. Start statements such as "you hope," "you need" and "you prefer" can be useful to add goal direction. What follows are our examples that include feeling, meaning, validation and goal direction.

You feel <u>devastated</u> because <u>Jenny was your best friend</u>. *My actions risked the loss of our relationship and ended your relationship with Jenny.* You need me to stay focused on our healing and understand the pain that I have caused you.

You feel <u>betrayed</u> because <u>you always perceived me as devoted</u>. *Our devotion to each other was always critical in our trust.* You need time to sort out if you want to stay in this relationship.

You feel <u>afraid</u> because <u>our future is uncertain now</u>. *It is important for me to understand how my actions make you fearful.* You hope that I can be consistent with keeping boundaries with people at work.

Resist apologizing when confronted on your behavior. Instead, accept responsibility to some part of the confrontation if you can. Too often, an apology for the hurt partner feels empty and overused. To take responsibility, acknowledge the behavior and then discuss the impact of this behavior to the hurt partner and to the relationship. For example: "Yes, lying to you about the text messages that I sent to her was wrong, and it makes it very difficult now for you to trust most things that I say to you."

"What's Wrong?"

You come home and you see a sad look on your partner's face, and you become concerned. You ask, "What's wrong?" Maybe you get the response, "Nothing." I would suggest that you respond to the mood state and engage your partner instead of simply asking "What's wrong?" I am sure that you can relate to this if you are struggling to put the pieces together after your infidelity.

To respond to the mood state is to state the feeling that you believe is associated with the facial expression that you are observing and invite discussion with your partner. For example, instead of asking, "What's wrong?" state, "You look frustrated. Would you like to take a walk and talk?" Another possible response would be to state "You look hurt, maybe you are thinking about what I said earlier." The second strategy attaches both feeling and meaning to the facial expression, which follows the example of empathy responding. Both statements invite discussion and engagement. Both lead to healing.

Managing and reducing triggering experiences is a slow process. Small moments of compassion can make a big difference for you and your partner. It can also increase intimacy, even during difficult times. It is better to be intimately engaged in talking about a difficult topic that to be disengaged and alone.

You have triggering experiences also. Though you might not feel this, it is fair to expect that your partner will help you with these. The power in managing the experience resides in both of your efforts combined. If you feel that you have recurrent triggering, ask your partner to learn and use the strategy of compassionate responding.

A Message for the Betrayed Partner

Your brain processes memory of traumatic events, such as discovery of infidelity, differently from other memories. The memory is not filed away as the event that is in the past but is cataloged as if it is in the present;

this is meant to help protect you from future harm. The brain also attaches details of the traumatic event to the memory so that if those details present themselves, you can quickly act to protect yourself. These details are triggers. Some details (triggers) are obvious, such as seeing a scene in a movie that portrays infidelity, but others are more subtle, such as the sight of a store or a restaurant. Anything that reminds you of the time right before discovery of the affair or during the fallout of the affair can act as triggers.

I would advise that you and your partner sit down together and identify the triggers each of you are experiencing. Yes, both of you, because my guess is that your partner has triggering experiences that you may not be aware of. Your partner may not be aware of what is going on with you either. A concerted effort on both your parts can ensure that both of you are in tune to the triggers that each of you have and are taking care of each other when things feel out of control or dangerous.

Early Prevention Is Key

I am hoping that the two of you will be purposeful in managing triggering experiences. It is best to implement strategies early so that the two of you do not get involved in strengthening an unhealthy pattern. Consider Pamela's description of the cycle she found herself stuck in with her husband. Her description demonstrates the strengthening pattern of Pamela's (1) intrusive thinking, (2) a behavioral response by Pamela, (3) her husband's uncertain or unplanned response, (4) her emotional breakdown and recovery. By the time the couple was ready for therapy, she said this about her triggers:

> These events are caused by intrusive, relentless images that I fight every day and most days, I overcome them. But he only sees the bad days and not the thousands of unseen victories.
>
> But the cycle, though longer, continues. The thoughts attack, I break down, and in the aftermath, we feel hopeless. Then, we talk and things are better. Until the next time – and we both live in fear of the next times.
>
> (Pamela, personal communication, January 8, 2018)

You may find yourself in a similar pattern. In Pamela's example, there are multiple places where this pattern can be interrupted, and needs to be interrupted. The first part of the pattern is intrusive thinking. For Pamela, her internal world was the trigger. In the previous chapter, I discussed strategies for managing intrusive thinking. Pamela was not using any strategies to manage the intrusive thoughts and believed that she was helpless in controlling them. Some of the strategies could have served as either prevention or intervention for the thoughts.

Pamela's behavioral response is problematic, but so is her husband's response. Pamela broke down, which indicated that she became dysregulated. She needed to find a way to maintain control and stay connected with her husband. In the same vein, her husband did not know how to manage Pamela's dysregulation and felt helpless. Had he compassionately responded, he would have been able to stay engaged with Pamela, and the couple could have managed the experience very differently. The power is amplified if both Pamela and her husband worked together as a team to manage the triggering experience.

> *For Reflection …*
> What is your pattern as a couple? What part of the pattern needs to be interrupted and changed to a healthier action?

Learn to know your triggers; it will help you heal and function better as a couple. If you have recurrent triggers, you might want to consider journaling them. As you journal, notice the themes that emerge. Are you able to identify the origins of those themes? As an example, if the theme is your belief that you are unlovable, where did that come from? Did you get that message from a parent, in school from a friend or maybe a past relationship? Evaluate that beliefs that are in the theme and challenge them so that you can adopt a more balanced and healthy belief, even if initially you don't believe it.

A Message for the Therapist

Triggering experiences are a common topic in treatment, and it is important that couples learn to manage them. An important strategy that will help you in aiding couples in trigger management is awareness of early warning signs and potential triggers. Discovery of early warning signs and triggers can help couples avoid trauma responses by being prepared to respond early to internal and external stimuli. Gillece (2014) identifies a three-step process for managing triggers as follows:

1. Identify triggers.
2. Identify the early warning signs.
3. Develop strategies.

My process is to ask the couple to identify the most common triggers. I start with the betrayed partner, but I will ask this of the betraying partner as well. Usually, the betraying partner will also have triggering events but will leave them undisclosed unless I ask.

Once the betrayed partner has identified the triggers, early warning signs are identified so that the couple can create early intervention strategies. Two categories of warning signs that I pay particular attention to are (1) the internal emotional experience that may indicate that the partner is triggered, and (2) observable indicators identified by the betraying partner. Each of these warning signs will be paired to interventions during treatment. Internal emotional experiences will be paired with interventions that can be implemented immediately by the betrayed partner on his or her own. Observable indicators displayed by the betrayed partner, such as facial expressions or withdrawing, will be use as cues to the betraying partner that immediate engagement is necessary to assist the betrayed partner.

I am an experiential therapist, and because of my theoretical orientation, I prefer to emphasize the importance of engagement during a triggering experience. My hope is for couples to have intimate healing experiences with each other even during moments of tension. There are a number of treatment expectations that I have around engagement, and for that matter, disengagement.

I suggest to couples that they should engage as soon as one partner notices the pain of the other. It's interesting to note that many times, either partners do not see the pain of the other or, if they see it, they do not act when they see it. When this occurs in session, I request that partners indicate that they see the pain and respond in a compassionate way. I ask couples to make this a priority at home.

There are healthy reasons to withdraw and unhealthy reasons. Most couples know the difference in their relationship. An unhealthy withdraw is when one partner becomes pensive and when asked about it, they respond by saying "Nothing." The response is congruent, and this congruency is recognized. I like to point out to couples that this is a common pattern. I ask them to look for this pattern and disrupt it though engagement and expansion of a discussion on the "nothing." As Edie Brickell aptly stated in her song "Nothing," "There's nothing I hate more than nothing."

Intrusive thought can draw people inward and lead to rumination. This is a form of disengagement with the present and with others. It is important not to feed the negative thoughts because if that occurs, it could be the beginnings of another session of rumination. Early engagement with the present moment through mindfulness experiences and engagement with others can interrupt the time for rumination.

Exploration of Triggering Experiences as a Between-Session Task

Table 9.1 displays a brief activity that couples can do at home that is similar to the topic that I have identified in the previous section. If time permits, sometimes I will do this in session as well. I ask each partner to identify one or two triggers. For each trigger, they will complete the categories in Table 9.1. Once each partner completes the items, I ask that they come together to discuss their responses and negotiate interventions.

Table 9.1 Identifying Trigger Experiences and Responses

Name the Trigger:					
Concerning This Trigger …					
My Emotional Experience is:	My Behavioral Responses are:	My Potential Avoidance Strategies are:	This is how others perceive me when I am triggered (Warning Signs):	Things I can do to manage this trigger:	Things my partner can do to help manage this trigger:

Bibliography

Gillece, J. (2014). Understanding and addressing trauma in the lives of those we serve. Retrieved September 19, 2014, from http://www.nasmhpd.org/docs/NCTIC/Joan_Gillece_SAMHSA_2012_updated_Trauma_PPT.pdf

10 Grieving in Isolation

Loss and grief are experiences that both partners have as a consequence of infidelity. You have lost something. With loss comes grief. We typically think of grief in the context of death. When someone dies, people typically come together to support one another, there usually is a funeral and memorial service, we participate in spiritual practices along with other rituals that symbolically connect us to experiences that are meaningful. We are able to comfort and be comforted, express our feelings and, through connection with others, bring a sense of closure.

This is not the grief you are experiencing. You are more alone in your grieving. You may be completely isolated. Friends and family may not understand the loss that you are experiencing. Your partner may not get it or may not want to talk about it. You may be uncomfortable expressing your loss to your partner or others because they would not be so open to hearing it. The type of grief you are experiencing is disenfranchised grief, which occurs when grieving is restricted in some way.

For Reflection …
In what ways are you unable to express the loss you have experienced? In what ways might your partner be struggling with loss and grief?

Disenfranchised grief can interfere with the bereavement process and your efforts to recover from infidelity. If you are not able to express your loss to others due to shame, uncomfortableness with the topic or unaccepting attitudes from others, you may try to repress or deny the emotions you are experiencing. Keep in mind that shame and secrecy can make the symptoms of grief more severe.

A Message for the Betraying Partner

You have experienced multiple losses, and the consequence of that is grief. You might believe that you do not have a right to grieve because of the pain that you have caused your partner. Yet, grieving is necessary to your recovery, and denying it will slow recovery.

You have lost the relationship that you were once committed to and relied upon. You have lost your partner's trust and confidence in you. You have lost the hopes, plans and dreams you had as a couple. As the affair developed, you lost your own sense of right and wrong and violated your own morals. The relationship has ended with the affair partner, and you have chosen to keep it that way to reinvest in your relationship with your partner. So, you have also lost the affair partner. With all this loss, you should expect to experience grief. Complicating it more is that this is disenfranchised grief; friends and family may reject your grief because they believe that you caused the problem, your partner may not be open to talking about your experiences because of his or her own hurt and pain, others may say you deserve it and there is probably no sympathy from anyone for the loss and grief over losing the affair partner.

As you work with your partner to repair your relationship, you will also need to be intentional in allowing yourself to mourn all the losses. If you do not take the time to do this, you will slow the affair recovery. Stuffing down your feelings never works.

Let's take a look at the four primary stages and tasks for mourning, specific to your affair. It is fairly complex because you are grieving the loss of your primary relationship that existed prior to your affair, and you may also be grieving the loss of the affair relationship.

Accept the Reality of the Loss

Take time to reflect on the significance to all that has occurred and the multiple losses that you have experienced. Identify for yourself all the losses that you have experienced. Accept that responsibility lies in your choice to have an affair and that there were personal and relational vulnerabilities that you allowed to exist.

Consider experiencing private, personal or spiritual rituals. This could be writing about the loss, listening to music, prayer or other things that are meaningful. This could be one-time rituals or could be weekly or daily.

Recognize that you may be grieving the affair partner. If you ignore this and do not work through it, you will likely slow your recovery with your partner. Understand that people may stigmatize your grief related to the affair partner and resist experiencing your grief alone.

Most of the couples that I have worked with are uncomfortable talking about this loss with their partner. They view these discussions as traumatizing to their partner. I tend to align with the point of view that it can be a traumatic discussion. Therapists also avoid dialogue about grief related to the loss of the affair partner, so you might not get much help in couples therapy. Connect with an individual therapist or trusted person to talk about this loss.

Work Through the Pain of the Grief

There is no correct way to feel when grieving loss. In this stage, allow yourself to experience the broad range of emotions that come with loss, such as sadness, anxiety, anger, loneliness, guilt and even relief. Show compassion and understanding for yourself, allowing the feeling to be fully experienced. Definitely do not try to ignore the feelings, but try to talk with significant others to create understanding.

Adjust to the Changes in the Relationship

Adjustment takes time. At this stage, you have disconnected from the affair partner and have a more balanced perspective of that relationship. You and your partner have a shared understanding of the affair, and you are working on correcting the personal and relational vulnerabilities. Your deeper work now is on the internal exploration of how you chose to have an affair. Your goal is to find a deeper understanding and connection with yourself. Your personal understanding will support you in developing new ways to reconnect with your partner in a more intimate way. Successful adjustment to new expectations and roles in the relationship will increase trust over time.

Reinvest in the New Relationship with Your Partner

Your personal understanding of yourself, your intentional choices and your relationship with your partner have evolved and are evolving. You have moved the energy from a triangular relationship of an affair and the task now is to create a strong investment in the health and vitality of your primary relationship. You will continually strive to meaningfully engage in the relationship with your partner.

A Message for the Betrayed Partner

Infidelity is loss, and quite a bit of it. You have lost the person who you thought had commitment to this relationship and lost what the relationship meant to the two of you. You have lost trust and confidence in your partner and the emotional safety that comes along with it. There is also potential future loss of the hopes, dreams and plans for your future together as a couple. You may even feel that you have even lost the sense of who you are.

Recognizing the losses associated with your partner's decision to have an affair and letting yourself grieve is critical to your successful recovery. Social support is an important component of recovery. In the previous chapter, I discussed the importance of selecting friends and family that can empathize and support your relationship. You were selective and choose someone who will protect your confidentiality, who will listen well and has good judgment. One of your selections may even include a therapist. Ongoing conversations with supportive people that are empathic and open, encouraging you to reflect on the multiple losses that have occurred, can be healing.

Even though grief is not a linear process, a number of tasks are indicative of healthy grieving. Let's take a look at the four primary stages and tasks for mourning.

Accept the Reality of the Loss

Take time to reflect on the significance to all that has occurred and the multiple losses that you have experienced. Identify for yourself all the losses that you have experienced. How are the feelings similar or different when you consider each of the losses?

Consider experiencing private, personal or spiritual rituals. This could be writing about the loss, listening to music, prayer or other things that are meaningful. This could be one-time rituals or could be weekly or daily. Work to accept that multiple losses are the result of your partner's choice to have an affair and that some of the loss may come from your own personal or relationship vulnerabilities.

Work Through the Pain of the Grief

There are many ways to experience grief. In this stage, allow yourself to experience the broad range of emotions that come with loss, such as sadness, anxiety, anger, loneliness, guilt and even relief. Show compassion and understanding for yourself, allowing the feeling to be fully experienced. Definitely do not try to ignore the feelings but try to talk with your partner about the emotions you are experiencing. Ask your partner just to listen and help you explore and make sense of what you are feeling. If your partner does this for you, it is the beginning stages of forgiveness.

Adjust to the Changes in the Relationship

Adjustment to changes in the relationship is an evolving process and will take time. At this stage, you and your partner have a shared understanding of the affair, and as a couple you are working on correcting the personal and relational vulnerabilities that have perpetuated in the relationship. Your goal is to find a deeper understanding and connection with yourself. Your personal understanding will support you in developing new ways to reconnect with your partner in a more intimate way. Successful adjustment to new expectations and roles in the relationship will increase trust over time.

Reinvest in the New Relationship with Your Partner

Your personal understanding of yourself, your intentional choices and your relationship with your partner have evolved and are evolving as you have worked through healing. As a couple, you have moved the energy in the relationship, and the task now is to create a strong investment in the health and vitality of your primary relationship. You will continually strive to meaningfully engage in the relationship with your partner.

A Message for the Therapist

In couples therapy, we tend to expect full disclosure of the affair relationship, including how the relationship started, elements of its development, the sexual experience and how it ended. The exception is disclosure of the loss experienced by the betraying partner for the affair partner and the resulting grief that occurs. Most therapists do not acknowledge this grief in therapy and, for that reason, tend to not have a plan to clinically address it. However, if it is not addressed, it remains a hidden force that will delay recovery for the couple. Therapists would serve their couples well by just assuming that there is grief for the affair partner and assessing the grief in early sessions.

The grief for the affair partner can be considerably strong if the affair was a long-term relationship, had deep meaning for the betraying partner or was sexually passionate. The grief can be compounded by the abrupt ending to the affair relationship, which happens in most cases. The betraying partner is thrust into balancing the struggle of the abrupt "death" of the affair relationship, which may have been enjoyable and carefree, and the immense challenges of keeping the primary relationship intact in the presence of significant pain and anger.

In my opinion, it does not make sense to do grief work regarding the affair partner in couples therapy. I could only imagine how appalling it would be for the betrayed partner to have to comfort and hold the hand of their partner as he or she worked though the loss of the affair partner. I get the interpretation that that experience could be traumatizing. Also, I worry about the message it would convey to the betrayed partner and how the partner might interpret their own self-worth.

I typically will refer the betraying partner to another therapist to work through this grief. This keeps me from the risk of hearing, and being requested to keep, secrets, which I guard against in my practice. I am aware that other therapists will combine some individual sessions with couples sessions, using individual sessions with the betraying partner to privately process the grief of losing the affair partner. I would suggest that you be careful to make sure the discussions were only about the grief and follow an outlined treatment plan that was negotiated with the couple prior to beginning any individual sessions. This will help you reduce the risk of the betrayed partner sharing any secrets that you would not want to maintain.

In the individual sessions, I would suggest normalizing the perception of loss and the many feelings of grief. I would help the betraying partner create awareness of their own self-focus and misplaced attachment. I would ask them to consider that their view of the affair partner may be idyllically distorted and encourage them to create a more balanced and realistic perspective of the affair relationship.

For the grief that both partners share, I would help them identify the many losses that have occurred and indicate that part of the emotional turmoil is grief related to the loss. Most couples will indicate quite a few. I like to point out that there is shared grief, hurt and pain that both partners are experiencing. In session, I encourage an open expression of the multiple feelings related to the losses and help each partner validate and empathize the feelings of the other. A common dynamic is that the betraying partner will share less about how they are feeling (disenfranchised grief), and the betrayed partner will express considerably more. The betraying partner may believe that they do not have the right to share their pain because they "caused" the problems.

11 The Revenge Variable

Revenge fantasies are common enough that most therapists view them as part of the healing process and, though it may come as a surprise to you, therapists tend to consider that they serve a psychological purpose. Revenge fantasies can decrease frustration and give people a sense of power and control. They can also be self-protective because the fantasies direct destructive impulses away from oneself. People that have been traumatized by someone can even feel good about having control in planning vengeance and may experience pleasure at imagining the suffering of the target and pride at being on the side of justice (Horowitz, 2007).

Of course, acting on the fantasies is a different story. When people act on them, they might initially feel pleasure and happiness but that is short lived. After the initial pleasure, the person will feel depressed and empty. If the person remains fixed on the revenge, it will limit their ability to foresee the consequences. It can also be a block in healing the relationship, and if you are in therapy, it can become an impasse in therapy.

Though there may be shame associated with revenge fantasies, I think that if you are experiencing revenge fantasies, no matter how severe, it can be helpful to disclose them to your partner or your therapist. Ongoing conversation about the fantasies may diminish their frequency and intensity over time.

A Message for the Betraying Partner

It can be very distressing when your partner tells you that he or she wants to hurt you or attack the affair partner. Your partner may also confide in you that they are experiencing thoughts of harm to you or someone else. I want to tell you that revenge fantasies are a fairly common experience, and I believe they can be a catalyst to healing for your partner.

As you know by now, many cognitive things are going on for your partner that, to your partner, seemingly feel out of control and irrational. Left unchecked, your partner can experience intrusive thoughts and revenge fantasies and move toward feverish detective work, stalking and exhibiting potential aggressiveness toward you or the affair partner.

Revenge fantasies are a message to you and to your partner. It is your job to understand the content of the fantasies and to discover the underlying message.

Knowing that some fantasy about hurting the affair partner or perhaps even hurting you are common, ask your partner if he or she has experienced any fantasies in this way. It will be helpful to normalize this for your partner and state that you recognize that the fantasies represent the deep wound from the infidelity. Help your partner express the content of the fantasies.

As your partner shares the content of the fantasies, focus your attention to the emotional aspect of the fantasies. Emotions tend to be either fear, hurt, sadness or shame. Sometimes emotions of happiness can be expressed about the possibility of getting revenge. This kind of focus will take effort on your part to see through your guilt and shame for a period to help your partner.

Recognize that your partner has not acted on the fantasies. Help your partner identify how they were able to resist acting on them. Support your partner in expressing the thoughts and ask your partner to keep communication open with you.

Know your own guilt and shame so that you can see through it and help your partner.

Anger as a Consequence of Infidelity

Allow me to take a moment to share a story to examine the topic of anger. When one of my sons was in high school, he came home with a beautiful piece of art that he created from scratch art. With scratch art, the artist creates a drawing by scratching off black ink that is on a white clay board, revealing the board beneath. His drawing is of an eagle that he titled

Before Flight. He generously gifted it to me, and now *Before Flight* is on display in my clinical office. Anger is like the coating that is on top of the board, when the surface is scratched, it reveals the complex emotions that are underneath it. Anger can be a veil cloaking these emotions. Under the cloak is usually fear, hurt, guilt or a sense of inadequacy.

Anger is certainly a normal reaction to infidelity, and your partner has every reason for anger. It is important to remember that our feelings find ways to protect us or drive us to action, which could help your partner push for safety in your relationship. Early anger helps create this momentum. As recovery from your infidelity continues, the anger will vacillate from anger to hurt and fear.

Understand your partner's anger. Empathize with it and work to understand it. As you work with the anger, also help move the conversation to other feelings that are around and under the anger, such as fear, hurt, devastation and sadness.

> *For Reflection …*
> What is one deep feeling (other than anger) that your partner is experiencing? How might your partner want or need you to respond to this feeling? Consider looking for times when your partner is experiencing this feeling and respond in the way that they want or need you to respond.

A Message for the Betrayed Partner

"It is so unfair. How is it possible that I have to bear so much hurt and by all accounts, [the affair partner] has had no consequences? I have all this healing to do and they get to go on with their normal life as if nothing happened." Following this dialogue comes potential ideas for creating more equitable consequences, such as contacting or sending a letter to the affair partner's spouse to disclose the affair, or confronting or even attacking the affair partner.

Revenge feelings are common and normal; acting on them is not. In truth, there are paradoxical consequences to acting on thoughts of revenge. There can be short-term positive results but also long-term negative consequences. Consider the couple R & C. The couple was recovering from C's affair when R abruptly re-connected with the affair partner. That evening, R called the suicide hotline to express feeling of devastation and suicidal thought, but admittedly did not disclose her revenge fantasies. Later that evening, she drove to the affair partner's house and, using her car as a battering ram, attacked C's car, destroying it. She came to therapy stating that it felt great when she was doing the damage. Hours afterward, she felt horribly guilty. Weeks and months later, she was depressed, had a high degree of isolation and feelings of loneliness and had begun excessive drinking in the evening. It took her considerable time to get back to a sense of stability and wellness. Fortunately for R, C agreed not to prosecute.

In my clinical practice, I routinely ask couples if there is any concern that either partner will hurt themselves or someone else. I like to open up a dialogue that conveys that these are concerning issues and also fairly common for couples experiencing infidelity. Ongoing discussions about the revenge fantasies can be healing because your partner can get a deeper understanding of the pain you are in, particularly if your partner is empathetic and compassionate when you share. I recognize that sometimes that is not possible, and you may need to work through this with a trained therapist who understand revenge fantasies.

If you are working with a therapist, share with your therapist that you have revenge fantasies. Since it is a part of the healing process, the therapist can help you process the feelings and motivations related to the fantasies. Sometimes the underlying motivation is not revenge as much as it is to save face, regain status, give a temporary sense of power or pleasure or reduce feelings of helplessness.

Your therapist can help you convey the deep pain of the affair to your partner and help your partner listen and respond effectively to this pain. These discussions can also help your therapist assess any risks that you may be presenting and get you additional help if needed.

Venting Anger

There are many reasons to be angry at your partner, the affair partner or even yourself. You may want to scream privately, punch pillows, lash out at your partner, vent your anger to your partner or some other way of venting to let go of some of the angry feelings. Some professionals will even recommend venting strategies as one of the better ways to resolve angry feelings, because these are considered a substitute, or "safe target." As it turns out, not much research supports venting (also known as catharsis theory), and quite a bit says it is not a good idea, that in fact it does not make you less angry, and it may actually increase your aggressive responses, even if you are feeling better after the venting. If venting is done on a regular basis, it is like practicing a bad habit, a habit of behaving aggressively.

One of the primary reasons that venting strategies can be counterproductive is that negative thoughts and memories are linked together in the brain, and when you are aggressive verbally or physically, you strengthen the neuro pathways that connect the thoughts to the actions. This makes future thoughts more likely to lead to aggressive actions.

Rumination

Rumination, the act of focusing on your angry feelings, can also increase the intensity of your angry feelings and increase the possibility of being aggressive toward someone else. Spending time thinking about revenge makes it more likely that you will be aggressive toward your partner or the affair partner.

Alternatives to Venting and Rumination

Here is an idea – do nothing! Considerable research shows that doing nothing is better than venting (Bushman, 2002), because venting fans the flames, increasing anger and aggression, and does not lead to a more positive mood.

To go further with the Bushman study, people who simply distracted themselves felt better than people who vented their anger or ruminated on their aggressive thoughts. I would imagine it would be even more helpful to attempt to reduce the angry feeling or aggressive thoughts than to just distract yourself, but the point is that doing nothing or distracting is better than venting.

Try meditating, practicing deep breathing when angry or even listening to calming music. Anger reduces faster when people take deep breaths, relax or just take a time out. Ultimately, any action that makes it impossible to sustain an angry state can help reduce anger.

A Message for the Therapist

In review of the literature on revenge fantasies, I have learned a number of things that have implications for couples treatment. For example, revenge fantasies have a potential positive function. People can derive a sense of satisfaction, decreased frustration and a restored self-esteem and emotional equilibrium by engaging in fantasies of revenge (Goldberg, 2004). Knowing that revenge fantasies may have some positive psychological function, we do not want to block the clients process completely because we might be limiting a part of the healing process. It would be better to hear the fantasies and work to interpret them and parse out the irrational beliefs or risky behaviors.

Revenge fantasies can also be self-protective and direct harmful thoughts away from self. When the betrayed partner engages in fantasy of revenge, they are not thinking about hurting themselves and there is also a positive emotional component of the fantasy that allows the fantasy to persist. As Mari Horowitz (2007) points out:

> The victim can feel good about gaining a sense of power and control by planning vengeance and may experience pleasure at imagining the suffering of the target and pride at being on the side of some spiritual primal justice.

Your couples may not want to tell you about these fantasies. They may perceive you as a secure base and that if they disclose their fantasies, they may risk their relationship with you or that they may be blamed for problems in the relationship (Morrissette, 2012). Their shame and fear that you will negatively perceive them can limit their willingness to disclose. The rage can feel extreme and even scary to your client, and they may fear that voicing the rage may even scare you. Consider the rage expressed by Donna (personal communication, June 14, 2018):

> I was hell bent on torturing her blonde, pigtailed ass. I sent her emails and texts and messages and mail every day until she replied. I sent her a copy of The Other Woman DVD. I mailed an enchilada cookbook to her apartment. I mailed her job openings overseas. I sent her a belated birthday bouquet of cake pops to the factory.

I included a note congratulating her on getting a new job away from the factory. I mailed a copy of a book about coming out as a gay man to her boss and signed it with her name.

I often comment that I would happily run over her body with my family minivan. And then I would like to back up over her body and run over her again. And maybe one more time for good measure. That's an exaggeration, of course. But I am not exaggerating when I say that I hope with all of my heart that her someday husband waits until she is exhausted from caring for their children, when her stretch marks are not just because she ate too many of my enchiladas, and then finds a girl half his age and fucks her in their marital bed. A lot.

All I can hope for, because I really don't want to go to jail for the other things I fantasize about doing to her, is that someday, 20 years from now, when she has stretch marks from her babies and she is too exhausted to shower, let alone have sex with her husband, that he goes and chases after someone half his age. I hope she one day feels all of the horrible pain she helped bring into my house.

Why should she get off so easily? She chose to do this to me. There was a time when I could have sued her for intentional infliction of emotional distress. Courts don't generally allow those cases anymore.

It is important for the therapist to assess for revenge fantasies and the potential for harm toward the self, the betraying partner and the affair partner. Victims tend to overcompensate for their injury and inadvertently promote a cycle of violence, and this potential is there even when the revenge response is mild (Boon, Deveau, & Alibhai, 2009), so we need to directly inquire about fantasies of revenge.

Revenge behaviors and fantasies are a challenging clinical problem for the therapist. The ways that the betrayed partner vengefully responds to infidelity is varied even though there are common categories of responses including verbal exchanges, physical aggression, reputation defamation, property damage, resource removal and ignition of initiation of new relationships. Also, it is difficult to identify the character traits of someone who may be vulnerable to revenge fantasies or behaviors. There is little research on the topic. We do know that men are more likely to react more destructively and aggressively in response to infidelity than women.

Treatment Considerations and Response to Revenge Fantasies

There are a few general strategies that you can do to be helpful in treatment. Encourage the couple to disclose if they are experiencing revenge fantasies and feelings of self-harm. Help the partners to understand that the thoughts of revenge are somewhat common and that they server several psychological purposes. If the revenge fantasies are present, assist the partner in interpreting the function of the revenge fantasy as giving them an illusion of power. It is important to help the partner differentiate the difference between irrational and rational beliefs within the fantasy.

Patrick Morrissette (2012) outlines a number of treatment considerations for addressing revenge fantasies that can be useful to help couples reduce fantasies and the risk associated if fantasies are allowed to persist. He sets two phases of treatment, which I will modify here. It is important to note that revenge fantasies could be focused on the betraying partner, or the affair partner or even someone who supported the affair. Discussions of revenge fantasies can also be accompanied by discussions about aggression toward self, such as suicide or self-harming or destructive behaviors.

Therapist Introspection

Before working with revenge fantasies, it is important that you have reflected on your own personal values regarding infidelity and how people injured by infidelity experience the pain. Secondly, having a strong theoretical understanding of the treatment protocol will positively influence your practice and the outcomes of the people you work with. Strong intrapersonal, interpersonal and clinical reflection will be important, and this can be done in supervision or consultation.

Fantasy Disclosure

Determining if the betrayed partner is experiencing revenge fantasies early and monitoring throughout the therapeutic process will be critical to the welfare of all parties involved and will help the couple help work through recovery. Disclosure has risk and benefits for both you and the client. Early discussions could start with evaluating the risk and benefits of disclosing revenge fantasies. One benefit from disclosure is that the betraying partner can have a deeper understanding of the pain that the betrayed partner is experiencing. If seated in empathy from the betraying partner, the betrayed partner may feel better understood. Disclosure will also help you to assess risks on an ongoing basis and the effectiveness of the couple's efforts to reduce distress.

Ethical Considerations for Fantasy Disclosure

The process of revenge fantasy disclosure carries ethical considerations for you as you begin to explore the content and intensity of the fantasies. You will need to be clear on your practice boundaries around confidentiality and duty to warn. In Ohio, where I practice, we have both a duty to warn and a duty to protect. Knowing your own professional ethical codes and laws governing duty to warn will help guide you with this difficult aspect of treatment. I personally tell couples that I will breach confidentiality if there is any plan to act in any way on the fantasy or that I have concern that there is any imminent risk. I recognize that this can limit the disclosure from the betrayed partner, but I also recognize that this is my legal and ethical duty.

Functions of Revenge Fantasies

Revenge fantasies are something that you should expect as a part of the recovery process. Helping the hurt partner understand that they are a common experience and your facilitation in uncovering the meaning of the fantasies are an important part of your treatment. Common reasons for vengeful thoughts include a desire to save face, regain status, give a temporary sense of power or pleasure, or reduce feelings of helplessness. Vengeance toward the betraying partner can be focused on teaching them a lesson, giving them a taste of their own medicine or not letting them get away with their infidelity.

Encourage the betrayed partner to identify how they have been able to refrain from acting on the irrational beliefs and emotional impulses. Support their efforts to self-regulate. Support their strength in restraint.

Paradoxical Consequence

Most vengeful behaviors fulfill a short-term desire. Following that, though, the result has a paradoxical consequence. Common emotional consequences of revenge behaviors (Yoshimura, 2007) are happiness, sadness, anger and fear. Individuals can feel shame, guilt or remorse from acting on their revenge fantasies. They may also feel fear of retaliation. After the initial pleasure of the behavior, the person often feels depressed and empty. Some people will remain fixed on the revenge, and this limits their ability or willingness to foresee the consequences of their potential behavior.

The Dangers in Venting Strategies

Some therapists may want to help the hurt partner vent their anger in an attempt to reduce revenge fantasies, and this is a misguided strategy. The well-intended advice a therapist might give is to punch a pillow or punching bag while thinking about the person who harmed them. The argument for venting is that if venting really does get the anger "out of your system," then venting should decrease aggression because the person is less angry. However, research shows that it actually can make the person more hostile (Bushman, 2002). As early as 1973, the famous theorist and psychiatrist Albert Bandura expressed concern about venting, issuing a statement calling for therapists to stop using venting strategies in therapy (Jennings, 2012, p. 215). Part of the reason for this is that the brain links aggressive thoughts together in memory and also links these thoughts to actions (Berkowitz, 1993). So, when angry thoughts are linked to venting strategies, such as punching a pillow, the network pathway from angry thoughts to aggressive action is strengthened, increasing the likelihood of other aggressive responses.

Therapeutic Techniques

There will be multiple versions of what the infidelity means to the partner experiencing revenge fantasies. A basic task is to find meaning and help the partner reconstruct their sense of helpless victimization and how it led to the restorative preoccupation with revenge scenarios.

A second task is to sort out the realistic and exaggerated beliefs in the revenge scenarios, including expected actions, responses and reactions. This could also include praise and condemnation from others as a response to fantasized actions and reactions. Making these fantasy scenarios clear will help promote differentiation between fantasy and reality.

A third task is to help the partner consider the extremes in their fantasy scenarios. You can help contrast beliefs about the demonized and idealized other and the idealized and demonized self. Reality can be found between the ideal and the demonized. The goal is helping the partner move to the center (Horowitz, 2007).

The following questions can be helpful in sorting out the partner's multiple meanings concerning the infidelity, separating reality and fantasy in the revenge scenarios and the fantasy and reality of the consequences of revenge action. Table 11.1 outlines questions revised from Mardi Horowitz's (2007) research on revenge fantasies.

In previous chapters, I have discussed that there are only a few occasions in which I would meet with one partner individually. At the consent of both partners, this would be one occasion that I would spend a number of sessions individually with the partner who is experiencing revenge fantasies. I would be particularly clear on the ethical considerations with both partners, particularly around my responsibility with mandated reporting and not keeping secrets.

Table 11.1 Questions for Differentiation Between Reality and Fantasy

Why did your partner do this?
Who was harmed by the infidelity (self, partner, children, family, friends), and in what way?
What was the context of the infidelity (who, what where, when, how)?
How much suffering for your partner would be enough?
What would be the likely consequences of your imagined retaliation?
How would you feel about these consequences of your imagined retaliation?
What are your values concerning (1) justice, (2) payback, (3) compassion and (4) forgiveness?
Under what circumstances might your revenge fantasies lose their emotional power?
What are alternative ways to gain a sense of purpose and meaning?

Bibliography

Berkowitz, L. (1993). *Aggression: Its causes, consequences, and control.* McGraw-Hill series in social psychology. New York: McGraw-Hill Book Company.

Boon, S., Deveau, V., & Alibhai, A. (2009). Payback: The parameters of revenge in romantic relationships. *Journal of Social and Personal Relationships*, 26, 747–768.

Bushman, B. J. (2002). Does venting anger feed or extinguish the flame? Catharsis, rumination, distraction, anger, and aggressive responding. *Personality and Social Psychology Bulletin*, 28(6), 724–731.

Goldberg, J. (2004). Fantasies of revenge and the stabilisation of the ego: Acts of revenge and the ascension of Thanatos. *Modern Psychoanalysis*, 29(1), 1–21.

Horowitz, M. J. (2007). Understanding and ameliorating revenge fantasies in psychotherapy. *American Journal of Psychiatry*, 164(1), 24–27.

Jennings, K. (2012). *Because I said so!: The truth behind the myths, tales, and warnings every generation passes down to its kids.* New York: Scribner (Simon and Schuster).

Morrissette, P. (2012). Infidelity and revenge. *Journal of Couple and Relationship Therapy*, 11, 149–164.

Yoshimura, S. (2007). Goals and emotional outcomes of revenge activities in interpersonal relationships. *Journal of Social and Personal Relationships*, 24, 87–98.

12 | **Erotic Recovery**

Erotic recovery is an interesting concept that is confusing to most couples. On the one hand, it can occur naturally in the early phases of infidelity recovery. This leads to confusion, fear and even frustration for some couples. Sometimes erotic recovery begins early in recovery but is short-lived, and the reasons for that can be misunderstood. If you are in treatment with a couples therapist, it would be helpful to review erotic recovery early in treatment to understand it and make it part of the treatment process when appropriate.

The function of the erotic part of the relationship is a critically important one. Your sexual relationship supports and is supported by your emotional connection. The affection that accompanies sex creates trust, relationship satisfaction and overall well-being. If the sexual relationship was never there for the two of you, it needs to be created; if the sexual relationship has been injured, it will need to be recovered. It is critical to the long-term viability of your relationship.

Erotic Injury

Erotic injury is the experience of shame and wounding that occurs for the betrayed partner that has a significant impact on the relationship. The betrayed partner can experience an undermining of erotic confidence, in which he or she has deep insecurity about the sexual relationship. This can lead to anger, rejection and the betrayed partner making comparison of self to the affair partner. Erotic injury can also lead to distressing triggering experiences and limit the ability for the two of you to erotically reconnect.

Erotic Recovery

Erotic recovery is an essential part of recovery following an affair. Following infidelity, your relationship needs the strength of an emotional and sexual connection. I know that you recognize that this is a complicated task. Yet, you will need to create a new sexual life together.

Interestingly, a renewed and intense sexual relationship following an affair is more common than you might think. Couples tell me that they have increased sexual interest in their partner, think about sexually connecting more and are "turned on" by their partner more than they have been in years. This can be very confusing.

My take on this is that erotic recovery is linked to the emotional connection and trust that increases between couples when they start to do the hard work following the aftermath of infidelity. The vulnerability of the emotional experience that occurs when you are struggling to make sense of the affair and the challenge to repair the impact draws you intimately close together and creates a great sense of vulnerability. This is a deep intimate experience, and it makes sense that all dimensions of intimacy will increase as emotional intimacy increases.

Erotic recovery can be short-lived, particularly if the emotional connection cannot be maintained. Some couples will have a strong emotional connection early on in recovery but find it difficult to manage the inevitable ups and downs of the triggering experiences and begin to emotionally disconnect and withdraw from each other. Stay committed to maintaining emotional connection and rebuilding trust between the two of you.

A Message for the Betraying Partner

You may believe that you are not free to express interest in sex with your partner. Your affair has hurt your partner's self-esteem, and you plan to wait quietly until your partner brings up the topic or initiates sex with you. I am inviting the two of you to have a conversation today about the importance of your sexual relationship and commit that at some point you will return sex to the relationship.

> *For Reflection ...*
> Consider your commitment to erotic recovery in your relationship. Would you be willing to commit to having ongoing discussions with your partner about the timing of reintroducing sex back into your relationship? Why is the sexual aspect of the relationship important to you, and how might erotic recovery impact the relationship? After reflecting, discuss this with your partner.

Your sexual relationship is uniquely tied to the emotional experience of your partner and the level of trust. Strengthening your emotional relationship with your partner and holding firmly to your commitments to trust-building behaviors will be important as the two of you reconnect sensually and sexually.

Strengthening Your Emotional Relationship

Your emotional intelligence can go a long way in healing your relationship and guaranteeing success over the long term. Emotional intelligence is the ability to understand, use and manage your own emotions in positive ways. It only makes sense that if you know what they're feeling, what their emotions mean and how these emotions can affect other people, you can help relieve stress and manage conflicts that are inevitable in your relationship.

Self-awareness is key to emotional intelligence. It can be helpful to slow down when you experience strong emotions. Give yourself time to consider what emotions you are truly experiencing and evaluate your reactions and any potential reactions. I have always noted in my own relationships that I tend to make less useful decisions when I respond with quick reaction in a state of strong emotions. Slowing things down and reflecting will lead to self-regulation. When you are regulated, you have more self-awareness and increased opportunity for intimate discussions with your partner.

With added self-awareness, you will be able to more productively work to understand your partner's perspective. Knowing your own emotions will help you to separate your emotions from your partner's emotions, a useful tool when trying to convey empathy for your partner. I would encourage you to notice your emotions and what they mean to you, and from this state of awareness, first work to understand your partner's perspective. As you do this, also convey your understanding of his or her feelings.

There will be times when your partner will be critical of you. Applying your emotional intelligence would allow you to hear the criticism, analyze it and, if the criticism is valid and intended for your personal or relational growth, hold yourself accountable to the criticism. That may mean stating acceptance of the criticism, in whole or in part, apologizing if necessary, and offering a commitment to do better.

Holding Firmly to Your Commitments to Trust-Building Behaviors

Previously, I asked you to commit to trust-building behaviors and for you to consider what it means to be a trustworthy partner. You shared with your partner your commitment to specific behaviors and attitudes that would help your partner feel emotionally safe in your relationship.

Consider now how those trust strategies might support the vulnerability your partner will need to sexually connect with you. Your partner may have problems with self-esteem, may make comparisons with your affair partner and may fear that having sex may be interpreted by you as things going back to normal and that you will quit working on the relationship.

Knowing that you are working on the historical problems in the relationship will also increase trust. Regularly talk about your progress in healing the relationship as a couple and engage in discussions about increasing the wellness of the relationship. Working with a therapist will help you in increasing focus by identifying the underlying problems in the relationship and establishing treatment goals.

Sensual Touch

There should be no pressure for either of you to have sex. Knowing that, returning sex to your relationship should happen sooner rather than later because the intimacy of your sexual relationship will bolster healing from the affair. Since there are a lot of things that you need to do to re-establish trust, create boundaries and recreate healthy connection, take the process of erotic recovery slowly. To help in slowing the pace, I suggest that you connect sensually with your partner before sexually. This means putting intercourse on hold for a while.

An excellent way to do this is through a process of sensate focus. Sensate focus is a way to practice connecting with your partner's body sensually, using all of your senses to experience non-genital touch with each other without intercourse. Sensate focus helps you re-engage sexually without pressure to have intercourse, helps the two of you communicate about what you enjoy in the sexual experience with your partner and strengthens your emotional bond.

As you read the next section, discuss with your partner if this would be useful to try out in your relationship. If you are working with a therapist, discuss creating a treatment plan that helps you specifically focuses on practicing sensate focus at home over a few months (or more) period of time.

A Message for the Betrayed Partner

There can be considerable ambivalence about reconnecting sexually with your partner. You may still be too hurt and angry to even consider the idea. In this case, it probably is too early.

Initially, it may be difficult to recover your own self-esteem in bed. You may feel insecure and believe that your partner does not feel that you are attractive. You may even compare yourself to the affair partner based on attractiveness, age, sexual interest or sexual behaviors.

It might be that your partner has not done enough to atone for what they have done. Being sexual with your partner may feel like your partner will be getting "off the hook" or that your partner may even think he or she got away with it. You also worry that if things will go back to normal, your partner may think all is forgiven.

The time to restart your sexual relationship might not be at this moment. However, I am inviting the two of you now to have a conversation today about the importance of your sexual relationship and commit to each other at some point to return sex back to the relationship.

I believe that retuning sex to the relationship would be best to occur sooner than later. I understand that a lot needs to happen for the two of you to recommit to your relationship after the affair, and deep healing takes time. However, if your sexual relationship is put on hold for months on end, it may slow the process of healing for the two of you. Consider the questions that follow and discuss these with your partner.

For Reflection …
Consider your commitment to erotic recovery in your relationship. Would you be willing to commit to having ongoing discussions with your partner about the timing of reintroducing sex back into your relationship? What are your expectations of your partner that will indicate good timing to reintroduce sex back into your relationship? What barriers currently exist, and what will eliminate or reduce these barriers? After reflecting, discuss this with your partner.

If you are ready for erotic recovery, take it slow. There should be no pressure to have sex. In fact, it can be better to take intercourse off the table for a while and develop the sensual aspect of your sexual relationship. In the following therapist section, I discuss using a process called sensate focus that couples can do at home, several times a week. Sensate focus is an ongoing practice of physical touching of each other's body, without touching genitals or breast, while disallowing intercourse, at least early in the process. As you read the next section, discuss with your partner if this would be useful to try out in your relationship. If you are working with a therapist, discuss creating a treatment plan that helps you specifically focus on practicing sensate focus at home over a few months or longer.

A Message for the Therapist

There are a variety of stage models for the recovery of infidelity. Tammy Nelson (2013, 2020) proposes three phases of erotic recovery that are in line with affair recovery.

Crisis Phase

The betrayed partner will commonly have intrusive thoughts about the affair and expect to learn the details of their partner's infidelity. Some couples will want to know all the sexual details while others will want to know less.

The couple might be having more sex with each other than ever before. The couple may be confused by this. Both partners may welcome the increased intimacy, yet the betrayed partner may worry that the betraying partner might interpret the new erotic nature of their relationship as "everything is forgiven." Since another person has intruded into the relationship, the increased sexual connection the couple may be experiencing may be occurring because of what Nelson describes as "mate guarding." It is a way to lay claim to one another when the monogamy of the relationship has been threatened.

Insight Phase

In this phase, the betraying partner has less focus on the details of the affair and engages in fewer comparisons with the affair partner. The focus moves to the emotional connection between the partners and understanding the multiple contributors of the infidelity. The movement is away from linear attribution of blame to a more circular understanding of the complex vulnerabilities of the relationship.

Vision Phase

The couple decides what the new relationship will look like. Nelson encourages couples to make a new monogamy agreement. This will include a new erotic life, one that is satisfying for both partners. This erotic connection will take work and will need consistent practice and commitment.

Sensate Focus

Some couples will ask for your help in revitalizing their sexual relationship. If the couple is presenting with a sexual disfunction, I will refer out to a sex therapist. If the request is related to erotic recovery related to infidelity, I will educate the couple on sensate focus and ask if they are willing to utilize the process over a number of weeks. The couple will also be giving an outline and timeline of the process and encourage to be consistent with implementation.

Sensate focus was originally created by Masters and Johnson as an intensive two-week treatment program for sexual dysfunction, in which clients were seen every day for two weeks, including weekends. This intensive format required social isolation to offer the opportunity for rapid progress (Weiner & Avery-Clark, 2014). The more contemporary implementation is in outpatient or private practice settings so that it can be more easily worked into the couple's daily life. As I begin to talk about sensate focus for erotic recovery from infidelity, understand that it can also be a great thing for couples who want to develop their sex life, even if there are no pressing issues that need to be addressed. It is a great way of enriching a couple's life and developing greater intimacy and ability to communicate desires.

Sensate focus is a nice way to activate sensuality and sexuality because it removes performance pressure by disallowing, at least initially, genital touching and intercourse. With sensate focus, the couple is instructed to create a specific time in the evening where they will explore physical sensual/sexual touch. The couple moves the focus away from intercourse, focusing instead on the range of physical sensations that can be elicited by touch.

The couple should try to do the exercises twice weekly for a month. They can start with 20 minutes per session and increase to an hour. There should be no talking during the exercise, with the exception of when touch is uncomfortable. After each session is complete, the couple can share their feelings about the exercise. The point here is that couples should stay focused on the here-and-now of the experience of sensate focus (Losey, 2017).

Stages and Tasks of Sensate Focus

Sensate focus moves through stages and has specific tasks (Fryer, 2010). These stages move the couple slowly through remapping the sensual experience of the partner's body and their own body. I ask couples to commit to two sessions weekly as they work through the stages. Each stage could last several weeks or a month before moving on to the next stage. This all depends on the needs of the couple.

Stage One: Non-Genital Touching

The couple should undress. One partner lies down to receive the touching, while the other is responsible for touching. This focus is on taking turns, touching the partner without intending to create pleasure for the partner but to enjoy touching the partner. For the partner lying down, they should just take in the experience of touch, without commenting or reciprocating. There should be no touch of genitals or breast and no movement toward intercourse. Continue with these sessions for at least two weeks, until you spend 60 minutes per session, or 30 minutes each giving and receiving. You should feel relaxed with a growing sense of trust and familiarity at the end of that period.

Stage Two: Genital Touching

This stage begins as in stage one with non-genital touching but can now move to touching genitals and breast. For the partner who is touching, it is important that the aim here is about exploration, not pleasing the partner. They should continue to focus on the other's whole body, not just their genitals.

The partner touching can experiment with different types of touch, pressure and friction and explore different areas of the body. The receiving partner will concentrate on the different sensations created through being touched.

At the end of this stage there is the option for mutual masturbation to orgasm. However, each partner is responsible for his or her own orgasm. This stage is not about one person having to give the other an orgasm. To support this concept, it might be better to start off with each person masturbating to orgasm in the other's company. This will help to make sure that performance pressure does not return.

Stage Three: Mutual Touching

In this stage, the couple can introduce mutual touching. Now there are sensations of touching and being touched simultaneously, adding complexity to the focus. Couple can move their attention back and forth. Still, in this stage, there is no intercourse.

Stage Four: Sensual Intercourse

Sexual intercourse is often a very mechanical act, with an emphasis on thrusting and pushing toward orgasm (Taylor, 2018). Sensual intercourse is different because it builds on the gains up to this point in sensate focus. Sensual intercourse can include insertion and includes the ability to fully engage in the sexual experience through all of the senses. If insertion does occur in this stage, it is recommended to avoid thrusting right away. Instead, the couple should remain still to feel the sensations that occur with insertion.

For gay and lesbian couples, this stage needs to be altered to include insertion of other objects, or entering into the mouth or anus as desired, or holding the genitals against the body of the partner. For example, a man may place his penis between the buttocks of his partner. This can also be a useful idea for heterosexual couples, as a lot of the time heterosexual couples can get stuck on the "penis-in-vagina" expectation (Fryer, 2010).

Processing Sensate Focus in the Therapy Session

To help couples keep the work of sensate focus consistently at home, it can be helpful for you to encourage processing of the sensate focus in your weekly sessions. Weiner and Avery-Clark (2014) suggests a number of questions to pose to the couple for reflection. Many of these questions might feel uncomfortable for you and the couple initially, but they can be very helpful in supporting the couple in discussing sensual experience and sensual preferences.

1. How many times were you able to do the sessions?
2. Who initiated each? How did you each initiate?
3. Can each of you tell me about the sensate focus sessions from your perspective?
4. What sensations were you able to focus on when you were touching?
5. When you were being touched, what touch sensations did you notice, and were there any differences from when you were touching?
6. What were some distractions, and what did you do to handle these?
7. Did you experience arousal and, if so, what did you do? What was that like?
8. Did you need to move your partner's hand away from something uncomfortable?

The Last Word on Date Night

Many couples will talk of their efforts at starting date nights to create romance and intimacy in their relationship. Some therapists will assign date nights. A few years ago, I attended the Treating Couples Conference at Harvard University (Harvard, 2018). At the conference Tammy Nelson, a board-certified psychologist, talked about therapists assigning date night for couples, which she argues against. To the laughter of the audience, she recommended assigning sex nights, not date nights. Her argument goes something like this. After couples have date night by going out for dinner, or watching a movie, they come home and are too tired for sex. Since many couples come in for therapy experiencing a problem with sexual desire, the focus is on getting the couple to re-engage the sexual aspect of the relationship. For couples wanting a more sexual and sensual relationship, skip advising date night, suggest sex night and help them engage in sensate focus.

Bibliography

Fryer, T. (2010). *A brief introduction to sensate focus* [workshop material]. Child Focus, Inc., May 6.

Harvard (2018). Treating couples conference. Harvard Medical School, Cambridge, Massachusetts, November 16–17.

Losey, B. (2017). *Creating an effective couples therapy practice*. New York: Routledge.

Nelson, T. (2013). Women who cheat: Understanding the message of the affair. *Psychotherapy Networker Magazine*, May–June.

Nelson, T. (2020). The three phases of erotic recovery after infidelity. *Recovery. org*. Retrieved April 6, 2020, from https://www.recovery.org/pro/articles/the-3-phases-of-erotic-recovery-after-infidelity/.

Taylor, E. (2018). Sensate focus: An old tool for modern intimacy. *Modern Fertility* (blog). Retrieved December 6, 2019, from https://modernfertility.com/blog/sensate-focus/

Weiner, L., & Avery-Clark, C. (2014). Sensate focus: Clarifying the Masters and Johnson's model. *Sexual and Relationship Therapy*, 29(3), 307–319. doi:10.1080/14681994.2014.892920

Reclaiming Strategies

A Message for the Betraying Partner

Your partner needs your help. There are places, songs and experiences that he or she believes are impossible to enjoy because of the affair. You are at a point in your recovery now that both of you need to take the power back from these situations. I call this reclaiming. Talk with your partner and identify what places and experiences need to be reclaimed and begin the process of systematically reclaiming them, reducing the power that these situations have over your partner.

I think it would be helpful for you to take the lead on this. The reclaiming process is basically to help your partner increasingly approach and experience an anxiety-producing event or location.

Approaching these situations requires considerable support from you. This means that you will go hand-in-hand with your partner through the process, both in reality and metaphorically. It is a shaping process that is done in a series of steps. Here is a story that will illustrate the concept. Consider how you can apply this process to situations that your partner is experiencing.

Rita, a 32-year-old mother of two, knew that her husband, Charlie, regularly gave flowers to his affair partner, shopped at certain stores for her, met regularly at specific restaurants, and took a "business trip" with the affair partner to New Hampshire the weekend after Valentine's Day. Rita felt powerless to listen to certain songs, drive by Applebee's restaurant, receive flowers from anyone or shop at Bed, Bath and Beyond. Driving by Applebee's or experiencing the smell of a specific store in the mall would be enough to activate great anxiety for her, crying and what she would describe as an emotional breakdown. She had written off ever visiting the state of New Hampshire.

Rita created a list of triggering places and events and then ranked them according to the level of anxiety they produced. Starting with the least anxiety-producing item on the list, she and her husband set out to experience each of these items together with the goal of reducing her anxiety with the experience.

One place Rita wanted to reclaim was the store Bed, Bath and Beyond. Here is their sequence of reclaiming:

1. Rita and Charlie walked in front of the store. Assessed Rita's anxiety on a 1–10 scale. Noted physical reactions of body. Did this multiple times until the anxiety was reduced. This took several attempts over several days.
2. Rita and Charlie sat in front of the store. Assessed Rita's anxiety on a 1–10 scale. Noted physical reactions of body. Held hands as a couple.
3. Rita and Charlie walked inside the front of the store. Assessed Rita's anxiety on a 1–10 scale. Noted physical reactions of body. Left the store. Did this multiple times on the same day.
4. Rita and Charlie walked inside the store, Rita tested the lotions, left the store. Assessed Rita's anxiety on a 1–10 scale. Noted physical reactions of body. Did this multiple times over several days.
5. Rita and Charlie walked to the back of the store and assessed Rita's anxiety as the couple walked through the store. Did this multiple times on separate days.
6. Rita walked into the store without Charlie and purchased an item.

Sometimes couples will use relaxation strategies during reclaiming. In this couple's process of reclaiming, they did not have any need to practice any relaxation techniques. My guess is that they did not push Rita to a level that the anxiety was high enough to experience intense anxiety. Relaxation could be useful with high anxiety. Having reclaimed Bed, Bath and Beyond, the couple came to therapy a few weeks later and disclosed they drove to New Hampshire and spent the weekend there. Reclaiming Bed, Bath and Beyond empowered the couple to take on more difficult situations.

> *For Reflection ...*
> What are the places or experiences that are triggering for your partner and need to be reclaimed? Consider taking the lead on discussing this with your partner and developing a plan to reduce the intense emotion associated with it. Do this by helping your partner gradually experience the anxiety-provoking situation with you, in the safety of your relationship.

A Message for the Betrayed Partner

Knowing the facts about the affair comes with a burden that some of the locations, people, songs and other things associated with the affair will cause anxiety and distress. Some of the anxiety can be paralyzing and can dysregulate your relationship, keeping you from going places and experiencing enjoyable moments. For example, it might be distressing to go to a particular restaurant because it somehow is associated with the affair. Even when you just drive by the restaurant, your heat races and your stomach churns. You imagine that you will never be able to go into that restaurant again.

You are in a place with your recovery that you can take back the power of these situations by reducing the anxiety associated with them. The process to do this is by slowly becoming increasingly comfortable with the experience. I have asked your partner to guide you through this process. The support will be helpful to you. It will also help your partner take a strong role in your healing.

A Message for the Therapist

Couples talk about the difficulty and distress of going to certain places, hearing certain songs and other experiences that are strong reminders of the infidelity. The typical response is to avoid the stressor. My process of managing avoidance are addressed in counseling both through imaginal and in-vivo experiences, both part of a broader treatment of exposure therapy. These interventions help the partner (1) confront situations, people and emotions associated with the stressor, and (2) identify, reorganize and neutralize environmental cues. I typically will begin with imaginal exposure experiences to help the partner confront his or her fears in the safety of the office. My goal is to help the partner to experience the feared thoughts more fully. Once this work is completed, I will move to in-vivo experiences.

Imaginal Exposure Experiences

Imaginal exposure experiences are in-office imagery, discussion and interventions that occur in the therapy session to address the avoidance related to the places and events connected to the infidelity. Most people want to avoid anything that reminds them of the trauma they experienced, but doing so only reinforces their fear. By facing what has been avoided, a person can decrease their stress symptoms.

Exposure to the stressful event through imaging allows the partner to experience the event in a safe, controlled environment while also carefully experiencing their reactions and beliefs in relation to that event. I start the reclaiming process in therapy with imaginal experiences. For Rita and Charlie, we completed several sessions planning the approach to Bed, Bath and Beyond and imagined the experience in detail before ever experiencing it out of the office.

In-Vivo Experiences

In-vivo experiences are the experience in which the couple "avoids the avoidance" by re-experiencing the place, song or other experiences outside the therapy session. In-vivo experiences use systematic desensitization, also known as progressive exposure, which is gradual and can involve gradual exposure coupled with relaxation exercises when anxiety levels become too great.

The person can take back the power they feel they have lost. They "reclaim the experience." Reclaiming is a highly structured experience. When couples begin the in-vivo experience, they have a clear understanding of how the experience will go. There is nothing left to chance.

An important element of the in-vivo experience is measuring the level of anxiety of the experience. I ask the couple to move forward in the steps of the process only until they have successfully reduced the anxiety in each step. They can use any measure of anxiety they prefer, such as a simple scale of anxiety from 1 to 10. Usually, I will connect the scale to body sensations so that there is consistency in measurement. For example, 5 = pressure on chest, 7 = nauseous feelings in stomach and so on. When the anxiety is high, the person can also use relaxation strategies to reduce the anxiety.

Another important component of reclaiming is partner support. Both partners experience all of the steps together. Rita and Charlie had a goal for Rita to be able to experience the store on her own. The final step in their process was for her to go into the store and purchase an item without Charlie. All other steps were experienced with him.

In-vivo experiences are distressing, but the payoff is empowering. When couples are successful with one experience, they can move to more difficult situations. Rita and Charlie were able to go on and reclaim a number of other places and even reclaimed a song that, for a long time, Rita could not even identify by name to the therapist.

Acceptance, Forgiveness and Reconciliation

14

To heal this relationship, it will require real forgiveness. Too often, people talk about forgiveness when we truly mean acceptance, so let us sort out the difference between acceptance, forgiveness and reconciliation.

Acceptance

Acceptance is the decision to take control and heal the pain when harmed by someone. With acceptance, we strive to come to an understanding of the injury when the offender is not available to us. You can hear examples of acceptance on the news when someone mistakenly states that they forgive the perpetrator of some crime against them, even though they have never talked to the perpetrator. This is acceptance. They have healed some of the feelings of fear, anger and retribution, but they have had no healing contact with the perpetrator.

Forgiveness

Forgiveness that will be transformative to your relationship includes two primary components. First, the betrayed partner will increasingly come to terms with the injury of the infidelity, and second, the betraying partner will stay involved in the healing process and help the betrayed partner. This will require the betrayed partner to soften the feelings of anger, reduce thoughts of retribution and punishment and reduce associated negative behaviors. The relationship will transform toward more positive experiences with the betrayed partner and feeling of empathy and compassion. The betraying partner will need to hang in through the difficult times to provide support, understanding and compassion. He or she will need to make considerable effort to seek forgiveness and acknowledge both responsibility and convey remorse.

Considering this, forgiveness is an ongoing interaction between the forgiving person, the offending person and the relationship between the two of them. It is not a product but a process, and therefore the continued work that you are currently doing is forgiveness.

Reconciliation

My personal view of reconciliation is that it is the next step beyond forgiveness. With reconciliation, a new relationship is born through movement to consistent positive experiences as a couple, one person has intimately sought forgiveness and expressed deep remorse, one partner has freely given forgiveness, and the couple has intentionally created a vision for the new relationship. For me, reconciliation is more than restoring the old relationship; it is the creation of a new and healthier relationship that is nurtured by both partners and grows more intimate over time.

A Message for the Betraying Partner

If reconciliation is your goal, the path forward can be a long one with many ups and downs. It will require your patience, your intentionality and a lot of goodwill from you and your partner. If you agree with my premise that forgiveness is a process and not a product, you will recognize that a number of tasks will need to occur in seeking and obtaining forgiveness. I will share some of these tasks with you, but I am not proposing that the process is linear. Many of these tasks will happen over an extended period of time.

Seeking and Obtaining Forgiveness

Obtaining forgiveness is more than offering an apology. In fact, many of the couples that I counsel state that the last thing they want is an apology. The betrayed partner will say they have heard the apology before or that they believe that the apology is insincere. Obtaining forgiveness is more than saying "I am sorry."

Taking responsibility for your actions may be more effective in seeking forgiveness. To take responsibility, state what you did that was wrong. This will need to be specific and could include a number of things. Once that you have shared this with your partner, talk about how your behaviors connect to your own personal failures in the relationship. How have you failed in creating the relationship that you had hoped for with your partner? How have your failures contributed to your choice to have an affair?

Forgiveness moves forward when your partner believes that you understand the impact of your decision to have an affair. Tell your partner what you know to be the impact of your affair for your partner, your family, your relationship, your children, you personally, your work and so on. As you share this, allow your partner to respond and really try to understand his or her perspective. Your partner's insights will help you identify other avenues for recovery. Make sure to demonstrate empathic understanding, reflecting the hurt, fear, loss or other feelings associated with the impact.

At some point, you will want to directly ask your partner to forgive you. This will help you move closer to reconciliation. Begin by stating your commitment to the future relationship. Help your partner see your vision of this new relationship and help him or her share their vision for the relationship.

A Message for the Betrayed Partner

Forgiveness is on a timeline, and you are already on that path as you engage in healing with your partner. There will be times that this will feel great and times where you think that you will never be able to forgive and move on. Sometimes you will feel stuck.

> To forgive is to set a prisoner free and discover that the prisoner was you.
>
> – Lewis B. Smedes

The Myths of Forgiveness

A number of things might keep you from considering to forgive or make it difficult to forgive. Sometimes when a person is having difficulty to forgive, they are ascribing to a notion about forgiveness that may not necessarily be true. A common myth I experience in the clinical setting is the betrayed partner believing that to forgive will lead to their partner disengaging from trying to heal the relationship or that there will be a loss in connection that has already been created. Forgiveness doesn't mean there is nothing further to work out in the relationship or that everything is okay.

Forgiveness is not pardoning the behavior of your partner. It is definitely not condoning the affair, nor does it mean that you should forget the affair ever happened. This happened, it was wrong, it caused great pain and it is an indication of deeper problems in the relationship. Since you have committed to stay together, discover the roots of the infidelity so that the two of you can make sense of it.

Forgiveness is not a single-moment event. When you experience forgiveness, it does not mean that you are relieving your partner's responsibility. As you continue to move through the process of forgiveness, your partner's responsibility continues, supporting you in healing. Forgiveness is not reconciliation, however. Reconciliation is the realization of a new relationship crafted by the two of you that is stronger, deeper and nurtured.

Forgiveness is not impossible.

For Reflection …
What evidence in your relationship indicates to you that you are already in the process of forgiveness? What do you need for your movement though forgiveness?

Considerations for How to Forgive

Forgiveness is a process that involves the two of you. You have been on that path for some time now if you have worked through this book or you have worked through the infidelity as a couple or with a therapist. Here are a few considerations that may help you continually move through the process of forgiveness.

Recognize Your Acceptance

Recognize that you have accepted that the infidelity happened and that you understand how it came about. Accept how you felt about it and how it made you react. In order to forgive, you need to acknowledge the reality of what occurred and how you were affected.

Make Meaning

Understand the pain in your relationship. Make sure to know the pain of the infidelity but also understand other pain that is in the relationship. Continue to work with your partner on making sense of things; true forgiveness progresses when you do the work together.

Create Empathy

Take time to examine some of the details of your partner's life that are not connected to the affair. Take a look at your partner's childhood, relationship with his or her parents, hurts growing up through the years and how he or she experienced other intimate relationships, and consider the hurts he or she is carrying in this relationship. You may come to realize that your partner was wounded and wounded you in return. This may help you start to develop empathy for your partner.

Acknowledge Your Growth as a Couple

You have survived the infidelity and in the presences of terrible pain, you have learned about yourself, your partner, and your relationship. You have changed many of the underlying problems in the relationship and have grown closer to each other. Recognize that though things may not be where you want them to be, your personal and relational growth continues.

Make Sure to Forgive Yourself

Recognize that you are a fallible human being and that there are hurts that you have created in your relationship. Be compassionate and forgive yourself, recognizing your intrinsic worth and goodness, despite bad actions. Forgiving yourself also prepares you for seeking forgiveness from your partner for the relational hurts that you have caused.

Make a Statement of Forgiveness

At some point, you will decide to tell your partner that you forgive them. Make this statement when and if it feels right. This will more than likely come when significant work has occurred between the two of you. When you say that you forgive your partner, try to make it an expansive statement that offers a deep understanding of the forgiveness.

A Message for the Therapist

A challenging task when talking about forgiveness in session is defining the concept. Though most couples in therapy may have a definition of forgiveness, their definitions rarely are the same. Some couples are reluctant to forgive because they believe that forgiveness will in some way let the other partner "get away with" their affair. Sometimes, the betrayed partner interprets forgiving as a way of absolving their partner of responsibility and as a risk to the future relationship.

Forgiveness is not the same as pardoning, condoning, excusing or even reconciling. You will need to be sensitive to the couple's understanding of the difference between the terms and clarify your own and the couple's definition of forgiveness. This discussion takes finesse in timing. If forgiveness is addressed too early in treatment, it may unintentionally be interpreted by the betrayed partner as invalidating the pain of the experience.

A common view of forgiveness includes the idea that forgiveness can occur in the absence of the person who caused the harm. It is not uncommon to hear a person on the news state that they have forgiven the stranger who attacked them. This perspective would suggest that forgiveness is an intrapersonal process, one that primarily resides within the self.

In other words, the victim forgives an offender and therefore has completed the process of internally changing for the better. This is actually not forgiveness. It is acceptance.

Transformative Forgiveness

There are a number of models of forgiveness. I do not believe that any one model best describes the forgiveness process that can occur in the clinical setting with couples who are engaged in recovery for infidelity. For that reason, my understanding of forgiveness in therapy needs to integrate a number of models.

One outcome goal I have for couples in my clinical practice is to experience transformational forgiveness and move towards reconciliation. The transformative forgiveness experience evolves; it is action. It occurs session by session, day by day. I would describe transformative forgiveness as a gradual and significant change that occurs on an intrapersonal and interpersonal level. Transformative forgiveness can be understood as an experience for the forgiving person, an experience for the offending person, and the changing relationship between the two of them.

The intrapersonal aspects of transformative forgiveness are an internal process for the betraying partner and betrayed partner. The betrayed partner heals through the reduction of the negative affective, cognitive and behavioral experiences. This is experienced by a softening of the feelings of anger, a reduction in the thoughts of retribution and punishment and a reduction of negative behaviors, such as unhealthy behaviors towards self or others. The betrayed partner attitudes switch to having more positive feelings of empathy and compassion for the betraying partner. Alternately, the betraying partner's internal process of healing will be experienced by acknowledgment and acceptance of their negative choice to have an affair, an understanding of why the affair occurred, a softening of the feelings of pain, guilt and shame and a desire to stop requiring personal payment for the affair.

The interpersonal aspect of transformative forgiveness requires a heartfelt participation in recovery from both the betraying and betrayed partners. Both partners heal by coming to terms with the affair and gaining more accurate beliefs about the relationship. The betrayed partner will express increased compassion and empathy for the betraying partner, as the betraying partner's behaviors will strongly indicate a desire for being forgiven. In the therapeutic context, the betraying partner would acknowledge responsibility and convey remorse, and the betrayed partner would offer an expression of forgiveness in a personal way.

As you can see, forgiveness is multifaceted, and the clinician needs a strong understanding to approach forgiveness effectively in therapy. Forgiveness encompasses cognitive, affective and motivational responses. It is transformative, in that it is the displacement of negative attitudes, such as anger and revenge towards damaging situations or people, with positive attitudes such as compassion and tolerance. Interpersonal aspects of forgiveness results in the betrayed partner coming to terms with the injury through a dedicated healing process with the betraying partner, which may lead to reconciliation.

Therapists' Concerns about Forgiveness in Session

Many therapists have three concerns when approaching forgiveness in therapy (Olmstead, Blick & Mills, 2009). First, it is important to understand the couple's view of forgiveness and use their language in the discussion. Using the couple's language can show respect and sensitivity to the topic and make it easier to address misunderstandings about forgiveness. This discussion includes assessing the couple's desire for the future of the relationship.

Therapists believe that psychoeducation is an important component to the treatment process. Two critical aspects of psychoeducation are: (1) helping clients understand that forgiveness is a process, and (2) facilitating client understanding of misconceptions regarding forgiveness.

The third concern is the concept of time. Therapists convey to couples that forgiveness is a process and that it takes time. Partners are typically in different places in healing, and the length of time for the process may be longer than what the couple expects.

Therapists are also careful in their timing of forgiveness interventions. It is important to assess the couple's readiness for forgiveness and wait for readiness before suggesting the option of forgiveness. There is the possibility that the clinician can broach the subject too early in the therapeutic process. One circumstance is when there is potential for further hurt in the relationship. Forgiving could be considered a questionable endeavor when a likelihood of further injury is possible.

Evidence-Based Forgiveness in Couples Therapy

Effective facilitation of forgiveness in therapy is not solely the responsibility of the clinician. Forgiveness is a multifaceted experience for the couple. The therapist can only create the context for transformative forgiveness for the couple who has a desire and willingness to experience the process. Effective interventions take into account both the clinician and the couple. What follows are a number of interventions that have support in the scientific literature.

Intentionality of the Couple

Forgiveness is intentional and takes effort (Younger, Piferi, Jobe, & Lawler, 2004). It takes hard work on the part of the betrayed partner. It will also take hard work and patience for the betraying partner. As with any intentional behavior, individuals need a compelling reason for their behavior (Ajzen, 2011).

The Couple's Belief that There Is a Benefit to Forgiveness

One compelling reason is the person's belief that the outcome for forgiveness will be a better relationship and will increase their personal wellness (Jeter & Brannon, 2015). It may seem obvious to mention this, but research also indicates that couples respond more negatively (i.e., anger and avoidance) when betrayed partners responded unforgivingly, and they responded more positively (i.e., benevolence and empathy) when betrayed partners responded forgivingly (Jennings et al., 2016).

Understand and Clarify Beliefs about Forgiveness

Effective interventions also incorporate the beliefs and attitudes of forgiveness that the couple endorses to help them accomplish tasks that they believe necessary to forgive (Thoresen et al., 2008). In addition, when the clinician is sensitive to the couple's language and understanding of their definition of forgiveness, it makes it easier for the therapist to modify the couple's definition and challenge any myths about forgiveness supported by the couple.

Facilitate Exploration of Benefits and Risks of Forgiveness

Effective interventions will also help people see the benefits of forgiveness for both their relationship and their personal well-being (Thoresen et al., 2008). Benefits of forgiveness include general health of the relationship, relationship longevity and satisfaction (Gordon, Baucom & Snyder, 2005; McNulty, 2008).

The risk of forgiveness should be considered, particularly related to behavior change of the betraying partner. The betrayed partner needs significant confidence that the risk to the relationship has been removed.

Assess Commitment to the Relationship

It is helpful to assess the couple's commitment to the relationship in regards to forgiveness. Some couples may want to work towards forgiveness and reconcile, while others may want to forgive and separate.

Planned Therapist Timing

Therapist timing of the discussion of forgiveness is crucial. If the topic is broached too early, the risk increases that the hurt partner will feel invalidated. This could stall treatment, or worse, could increase the likelihood that the couple will drop out of treatment.

Reduce Negative Emotional, Cognitive, Behavioral and Motivational Experiences

Couples also need an emotional compelling reason to change. Effective interventions for couples tend to target prosocial change within the relationship and generally encourage the reduction of negative emotions, such as anger, hostility, and blame (Thoresen et al., 2008).

Encourage Empathy and Patience

The clinician can encourage the betraying partner to practice empathy for the betrayed partner. This takes effort and patience. Oftentimes both partners are on different timelines for healing and forgiveness, and healing will be a slow process.

The timeline for healing and forgiveness can be explained this way: The betrayed partner is working through a slow process of making sense of things, and the betraying partner is moving a bit more quickly to move the relationship to a new place of relationship functioning. Patience is needed to allow for this process.

Bibliography

Abrahms Spring, J. (2004). *How can I forgive you?* New York: HarperCollins Publishers.

Ajzen, I. (2011). The theory of planned behavior: Reactions and reflections. *Psychology and Health*, 26, 1113–1127.

Baucom, D. H., Gordon, K. C., Snyder, D. K., Atkins, D. C., & Christensen, A. (2006). Treating affair couples: Clinical considerations and initial findings. *Journal of Cognitive Psychotherapy: An International Quarterly*, 20 (4), 375–392.

Burnette, J. L., Davis, D. E., Green, J. D., Worthington, E. L., Jr., & Bradfield, E. (2009). Insecure attachment and depressive symptoms: The mediating role of rumination, empathy, and forgiveness. *Personality and Individual Differences*, 46, 276–280.

Chung, M. S., & Lee, K. J. (2014). A path-analytic study of associations between attachment, rumination, empathy, and forgiveness. *Journal of Special Education and Rehabilitation Science*, 53, 193–209.

DiBlasio, F. A., & Brenda, B. B. (2008). Forgiveness intervention with married couples: Two empirical analysis. *Journal of Psychology and Christianity*, 27(2), 150–158.

Enright, R. D., & Fitzgibbons, R. P. (2000). *Helping clients forgive: An empirical guide for resolving anger and restoring hope.* Washington, DC: APA Books. doi:10.1037/10381-000.

Fife, S., Weeks, G., & Stellberg-Filbert, J. (2013). Facilitating forgiveness in the treatment of infidelity: An interpersonal model. *Journal of Family Therapy*, 35(4), 343–367.

Finkel, E. J., Rusbult, C. E., Kumashiro, M., & Hannon, P. A. (2002). Dealing with betrayal in close relationships: Does commitment promote forgiveness? *Journal of Personality and Social Psychology*, 82, 956–974.

Gordon, K. C., & Baucom, D. H. (2003). Forgiveness and marriage: Preliminary support for a measure based on a model of recovery from a marital betrayal. *The American Journal of Family Therapy*, 31, 179–199.

Gordon, K., Baucom, D. H., & Snyder, D. K. (2005). Forgiveness in couples: Divorce, infidelity, and couples therapy. In E. L. Worthington (Ed.), *Handbook of forgiveness* (pp. 407–421). New York: Routledge.

Jennings, D. J., II, Worthington, E. L., Jr., Van Tongeren, D. R., Hook, J. N., Davis, D. E., Gartner, A. L., ... Mosher, D. K. (2016). The transgressor's response to denied forgiveness. *Journal of Psychology and Theology*, 44(1), 16–27.

Jeter, W. K., & Brannon, L. A. (2015). Increasing awareness of potentially helpful motivations and techniques for forgiveness. *Counseling and Values*, 60, 186–200.

Kearns, J. N., & Fincham, F. D. (2004). A prototype analysis of forgiveness. *Personality and Social Psychology Bulletin*, 30, 838–855.

Maltby, J., Macaskill, A., & Day, L. (2001). Failure to forgive self and others: A replication and extension of the relationship between forgiveness, personality, social desirability and general health. *Personality and Individual Differences*, 30, 881–885. doi:10.1016/S0191-8869(00)00080-5.

McCullough, M. E., Rachal, K. C., Sandage, S. J., Worthington, E. L., Jr., Brown, S. W., & Hight, T. L. (1998). Interpersonal forgiving in close relationships II: Theoretical elaboration and measurement. *Journal of Personality and Social Psychology*, 75, 1586–1603.

McNulty, J. K. (2008). Forgiveness in marriage: Putting the benefits into context. *Journal of Family Psychology*, 22, 171–175. http://doi.org/c8tmt8.

Myung-Sun, C. (2016). Relation between lack of forgiveness and depression: The moderating effect of self-compassion. *Psychological Reports*, 119(3), 573–585. doi:10.1177/0033294116663520.

Olmstead, S. B., Blick, R. W., & Mills, L. I. (2009). Helping couples work toward the forgiveness of marital infidelity: Therapists' perspectives. *The American Journal of Family Therapy*, 37, 48–66. doi:10.1080/01926180801960575.

Paleari, G. F., Regalia, C., & Fincham, F. (2005). Marital quality, forgiveness, empathy and rumination: A longitudinal study. *Personality and Social Psychology Bulletin*, 31(3), 368–378.

Sells, J. N., & Hargrave, T. D. (1998). Forgiveness: A review of the theoretical and empirical literature. *Journal of Family Therapy*, 20, 21–36.

Thoresen, C. E., Harris, A. H., & Luskin, F. (2000). Forgiveness and health: An unanswered question. In M. E. McCullough, K. I. Pargament, & C. E. Thoresen (Eds.), *Forgiveness: Theory, research, and practice* (pp. 254–280). New York: Guilford Press.

Thoresen, C. E., Luskin, F., & Harris, A. H. (2008). Science and forgiveness interventions: Reflections and recommendations. *Dimensions of Forgiveness: A Research Approach*, 1, 163–190.

Yarhouse, M. A., Atkinson, A., & Hefner, W. G. (2015). A longitudinal study of forgiveness and post-disclosure experience in mixed orientation couples. *The American Journal of Family Therapy*, 43, 138–150. doi:10.1080/01926187.2014.956628.

Younger, J. W., Piferi, R. L., Jobe, R. L., & Lawler, K. A. (2004). Dimensions of forgiveness: The views of laypersons. *Journal of Social and Personal Relationships*, 21, 837–855.

15

Selecting a Therapist for the Two of You

It is possible that this book is not enough. You may find that you need a therapist to help you in your recovery. One mistake I see that couples make regularly when entering therapy is choosing a therapist just because they are listed on their insurance plan. They choose the therapist that is on their plan, close to home, and they assume that the therapist knows how to do couples therapy and infidelity treatment. And this is likely not the case.

Bad Couples Therapy

How do you know the good therapists? Maybe it would help to know what is considered bad therapy? William Doherty (2002) talks about the challenge of receiving quality couples therapy in his article "Bad Couples Therapy: Betting Past the Myth of Therapist Neutrality" in *Psychotherapy Networker*:

> A dirty little secret in the therapy field is that couples therapy may be the hardest form of therapy, and most therapists aren't good at it. Of course, this wouldn't be a public health problem if most therapists stayed away from couples work, but they don't. Surveys indicate that about 80 percent of therapists in private practice do couples therapy. Where they got their training is a mystery, because most therapists practicing today never took a course in couples therapy and never did their internships under supervision from

someone who'd mastered the art. From a consumer's point of view, going in for couples therapy is like having your broken leg set by a doctor who skipped orthopedics in medical school.

Couples Therapy Is Different and Difficult

Usually couples therapy starts from a very fragile place. One or both partners may be ambivalent about staying in the relationship or uncertain that change can even occur. Many couples begin therapy with the threat of breaking up. Tension is high, and there is hyper-sensitivity to specific issues. There is a risk that rapid escalation can occur at any moment, and if the therapist is not structured, the session can devolve to an unhealthy place before the therapist can have a chance to intervene.

Good Couples Therapy

Good couples therapy will start with the establishment of a strong therapeutic alliance. Without early development of the therapeutic alliance, couples seeking treatment will tend to move on to another therapist. Many studies have been done that show that the qualities of the therapist are more important than the theory and techniques that they use. It is important, then, that your therapist be someone that you can create a strong connection with, who is focused on you and your needs and is someone that can be authentic and genuine. Following are a few other characteristics of an effective couples therapist.

The Therapist Will Help You Alter Your View of the Relationship

Throughout the therapeutic process, the therapist will attempt to help both of you see the relationship in a more objective manner rather than one-sided and blaming. It may be difficult for you to fully recognize that your own behaviors contribute to the relationship problems. Therapy should help you understand that the problems, and the solutions, are mutually created dynamics between the two of you.

The Therapist Will Help You Modify Dysfunctional Behavior

Good therapy helps change the way the two of you behave with one another. This means that in addition to helping you improve your interactions, therapists also need to ensure that couples are not engaging in actions that can cause physical or psychological harm. It is helpful when the couples therapist offers good structure and sets boundaries for the session. The last thing you want is to have a therapist who does not control the interaction between the two of you and allows anything to happen in session.

The Therapist Will Help You Reduce Emotional Avoidance

When couples avoid expressing their private thoughts and feelings to each other, this puts them at greater risk of becoming emotionally distant and will grow apart. This emotional distance tends to support dysfunctional communication patterns, such as one partner pushing for change and the other partner withdrawing. A good therapist will disrupt these patterns and ask each partner to share emotions and thoughts, opening up the perspectives of each partner.

The Therapist Will Help You Improve Communication

Most couples come to therapy saying that they have problems communicating. A therapist should be able to help you understand a healthy communication process and challenge you to discontinue unhealthy communication in session. Early in therapy, the therapist will likely teach communication strategies that create intimacy, improve listening skills and reduce defensiveness. A good therapist will also take a coaching approach with you to help you successfully navigate difficult conversations. Most couples in therapy will need to be encouraged to create vulnerability in disclosure and may need help in responding to disclosures in appropriate ways. These can be guided in-session experiences, called enactments. These experiences can open up conversations that have been avoided for a long time and reduce resentments in the relationship.

The Therapist Will Help You Utilize Your Strengths

Couples therapy often focuses on difficulties in the relationship but successful couples therapy does not end with just removal of the identified problems. A good couples therapist will help you develop a more deeply satisfying relationship sustainable from the perspective of both of you. Helping you focus on the strengths and the good aspects of the relationship will increase the likelihood that you will enjoy the relationship.

The Therapist Moderates, Controls and Facilitates Discussion

You should do more than just talk to your therapist in therapy. Talking to the therapist in couples therapy, if constructed intentionally by the therapist, is considered filtered dialogue. Filtered dialogue is used early in treatment to learn about the couple and at other times in therapy, for example, to regulate emotions during the discussion. A good portion of the discussion in therapy should be between the two of you, with the therapist coaching the process.

Selecting a Good Couples Therapist

Choosing a therapist just because they are close to your home, because they are the least expensive or because they are listed on your insurance plan can be a significant mistake. The result will likely be that you will select a therapist who is close to your home, is cheaper than other therapists and is someone who takes insurance.

> Choosing a therapist because they are close to your home,
> the least expensive or listed on your insurance plan
> will likely result in selecting a therapist who is
> close to your home,
> is cheaper than other therapists
> and is someone who takes insurance.

The problem with selecting a therapist this way is that you are needing a couples therapist who can help you recover from infidelity, not an inexpensive therapist close to home. A better selection process is a choice based on the therapist's specialization, clinical skills, years of experience and reputation for getting positive results.

The therapist will need to have two broad sets of competencies. First, they will need to have training and experience in couples therapy. Second, they need to have training and experience in infidelity treatment. Without these competencies, the therapist is ill-equipped to help you and may cause more harm than help.

Where to Find a Good Recommendation for a Couples Therapist

Most couples therapists are in private practice settings. There are a number of good ways to connect with a couples therapist. Many of these therapists list their practice on paid websites such as psychologytoday.com or goodtherapy.org. Be careful, though; many therapists try to throw out a large net to capture as many clients as possible. Look for a therapist that has the competencies that I have mentioned and one who can demonstrate considerable experience working with couples recovering from infidelity.

Ask other therapists! Maybe you are currently in individual therapy and you could ask your therapist. Though there are a large number of therapists in most communities, specialist in couples therapy and infidelity treatment are usually known by other therapists. Good couples therapists have a reputation for being a good therapist with past clients and therapists in the professional community.

Clergy members can assist in helping you find a good couples therapist. Many maintain a list of potential referrals for a variety of specialties. Many have close professional relationships with couples therapists.

Vetting the Recommended Therapist

Review the Therapist's Website and Online Presence

Identify the therapist's educational and training background. Make sure they have training in couples therapy and experience with infidelity treatment. Check to see if they are new to the field or if they have years of experience. You can check out their license on the licensing board website for your state to learn how long the therapist has been licensed and if they have been disciplined in any way for problematic behavior. You can also read reviews on Google, but these reviews are not always reflective of the therapist and may reflect personal characteristics of the reviewer. Look for themes in the reviews to have a more accurate picture.

Contact the Therapist

A therapist should be accessible to talk with you prior to setting up an appointment. You should expect that the therapist would be willing to talk with you, answer your questions and give you a good sense of who they are and how they work with couples. Ask the therapist to talk with you about how they help couples recover from infidelity. If they are unable to, it is an indication that they do not have the professional competencies in infidelity treatment.

Bibliography

Doherty, W.J. (2002). Bad couples therapy: Betting past the myth of therapist neutrality. *Psychotherapy Networker*, November–December, pp. 26–33.

16 | Ethical and Legal Considerations for Couples Therapy

Adherence to professional ethics, state and federal law, accepted clinical practice and common professional values will create the foundation for the therapist to provide effective treatment. This chapter is not meant to offer an exhaustive review of law and ethics related to couples therapy, but more so a review of common issues that a couples therapist might encounter in their therapy practice.

Common Ethical Considerations for Couples Therapy

There are two concepts that therapists tend to use interchangeably but have very different meanings; these are scope of practice and competency. Scope of practice is legally defined and in the United States is regulated through state boards. Competency is the product of education, training and supervised experience. So, it is possible to have scope of practice but not competency, which would be a violation of ethical practice if the therapist is practicing couples therapy without supervision. As an example, a therapist may have the legal right to practice couples therapy because it is within their licensure's scope of practice; without training and supervision on couples therapy, they would not have competency. For that reason, just having a license to practice does not mean that therapists can practice couples therapy. They would also need the education, training and supervised experience. These concepts also apply to infidelity treatment. Therapists need to make sure that they have scope of practice and the competencies of both couples therapy and infidelity treatment.

Two basic ethical responsibilities are beneficence, which is the therapist's efforts to do good on the client's behalf, and non-malfeasance, which is the therapist's obligation to interact with the client without doing harm. Alarmingly, infidelity treatment and couples therapy are quite commonly practiced by therapists with little or no specific training. It is highly important that therapists get additional training and supervision if they are interested in working with couples. Additional training should include developing skills to work with severe attachment disruptions, violence and abuse, sexual concerns and high conflict, just to name a few. Infidelity treatment has an added complexity. Therapists will need to know that infidelity treatment requires a specific protocol and have the skills to manage disruption in trust, relational boundaries, therapeutic boundaries, crisis intervention and trauma. These issues make couple counseling with infidelity as the primary concern highly complex and specialized. Without this training, there is great risk of not offering the best service to the client (beneficence) and, worse, causing harm to the couple (malfeasance).

Neutrality

Therapists want to believe they are neutral, but in truth, they are not. Therapists may have strong beliefs about healthy relationships, the process of change, beliefs about love, intimacy and sexuality and what constitutes appropriate communication patterns. These beliefs will guide their work with couples. There are also times when neutrality may not be appropriate; for example, in situations in which one partner's behavior is hurting the relationship or hurting the other partner.

Though the therapist is not neutral, they can work to be multi-perspective. A multi-perspective therapist will consider the perspective of both partners and their own perspective. In doing so, they may help create new awareness for the couple, generate perspective-taking between the partners and offer new possibilities for solutions that may not have been considered by the couple.

Individual Sessions

Sometimes, therapists may occasionally arrange to see one or both partners individually. If therapists choose to do so, there must be a clear and strong clinical rationale. There are three clinical reasons that therapists may consider individual sessions in the context of couples therapy (Weeks, Odell, & Methven, 2005). First, it may be that one partner needs to share information that might be hurtful to the other partner. In this case, having an individual session to plan for the disclosure in an upcoming session can be helpful in considering the best way to share the information. Second, the therapist may believe that one partner may need to bond more with the therapist. This could occur when one partner has high levels of defensiveness with the therapist, possibly because of not trusting or "believing in" therapy. A third reason would be when the therapist suspects that a secret is being hidden, in which the secret is inhibiting progress. In these cases, the therapist may work to uncover the secret and help the partner facilitate disclosure of the secret, if discovered. Sometimes, the partner may state that there is a secret and ask for help to disclose it.

It is important that the therapist consider the consequences of the decision to see the couple individually, even before discussing the possibility with the couple. Usually, to avoid a conflict of interest, these sessions are conducted under the rule that there will be no secrets and anything spoken in the individual sessions can be brought back to the couples session. Secondly, once confidentiality and parameters of the individual sessions are discussed, it is important to have both partners in agreement before proceeding.

Confidentiality and Informed Consent

Confidentiality is the foundation of effective therapy and is one of the most important aspects of informed consent. In couples counseling, the therapist is required to clearly define who is considered "the client" and discuss expectations and limitations of confidentiality. I clearly explain to the couple that "the relationship" is my client and therefore, I am guided by what is best for my client, which is the relationship.

This is true for confidentiality as well. We are expected to document in writing the agreement among all involved parties regarding the confidentiality of information. Confidentiality is covered in my standard informed consent paperwork, but I also have an additional process of detailing my policy on how I will manage secrets – in other words, how I will deal with one partner privately sharing information to me and requesting that I not share it with the other partner. My particular take on this issue is that I prefer not to keep secrets and try to not put myself in the situation of needing to do so. For that reason, I have a no-secrets policy. You will need to decide how you will deal with secrets in therapy.

Many therapists have a no-secrets policy and believe that this protects them from violating confidentiality when providing individual sessions. It does not. It only protects them from having an unhappy couple when they share information from the individual session to the couples session. A no-secrets policy is sufficient in offering informed consent about the management of secrets but not sufficient for disclosing a secret of one partner, shared in confidence to the therapist, to the other partner. The American Association of Marriage and Family Therapy directly states in their code of ethics, Section 2.2: "In the context of couple, family or group treatment, the therapist may not reveal any individual's confidences to others in the client unit without the prior written permission of that individual" (AAMFT, 2017).

For this reason, I recommend a policy and consent statement as part of a no-secrets policy that includes an authorization for release of information from the individual sessions back to the couples session. This release should cover a written agreement that allows disclosure to each partner all of the communication in individual sessions because the individual sessions are to be considered part of the couples treatment. Authorized disclosure would include information obtained in individual sessions but also individual communications, such as any phone calls, emails and text from one partner to the therapist. If the couple does not authorize the release of information from individual sessions, I would refrain from using individual sessions as part of couples therapy.

The following is an outline of information in my no-secrets policy that I believe are important for informed consent and authorization for release. Certainly, make sure to review this with your own attorney to consider applicable laws in your professional discipline and state of practice.

No-Secrets Policy

Policy Statement 1: The Couple is the Client

This written policy is intended to inform you, the participants in therapy, that when I agree to treat a couple, I consider the couple to be my client (the treatment unit). For this reason, my responsibility for confidentiality is to the couple, not just the individual.

These sessions are confidential and I will not release any confidential information to a third party unless I am required by law to do so or unless I have written authorization from all members of the treatment unit.

For instance, if there is a request for the treatment records of the couple, I will seek the authorization of all members of the treatment unit before I release confidential information to third parties. If any member of the treatment unit refuses authorization to release information, I will decline to do so. Also, if my records are subpoenaed, I will assert the counselor-client privilege on behalf of the client, which is the treatment unit.

Policy Statement 2: Management of Individual Sessions and Other Communication

During the course of my work with a couple, I may see one of you individually for one or more sessions. Though individual sessions are rare in my practice, these sessions should be seen by you as a part of the work that I am doing with you as a couple. In addition, any communication with me outside of the couple session should be considered part of the couple treatment.

Policy Statement 3: Management of Communication

At some point, I may need to share information learned from you or your partner in an individual session (or other communication outside the couples session) with the entire treatment unit (the couple) if I am to effectively serve the unit being treated. I will use my best judgment as to whether, when and to what extent I will make disclosures to the treatment unit. I will also, if appropriate, first give the individual or the smaller part of the treatment unit the opportunity to make the disclosure. Thus, if you feel it necessary to talk about matters that you absolutely want to be shared with no one, you might want to consult with an individual therapist who can treat you individually.

This "no-secrets" policy is intended to allow me to continue to treat the couple by preventing, to the extent possible, a conflict of interest to arise where an individual's interests may not be consistent with the interests of the unit being treated. For instance, information learned in the course of an individual session may be relevant or even essential to the proper treatment of the couple. If I am not free to exercise my clinical judgment regarding the need to bring this information to the couple during their therapy, I might be placed in a situation where I will have to terminate treatment of the couple. This policy is intended to prevent the need for such a termination.

Policy Statement 4: Consent and Authorization for Release

I, _____ (Client Name), acknowledge by my signature below, that I have read this policy, that I understand it, that I have had an opportunity to discuss its contents with Dr. Butch Losey. Ed.D., PCC-S and that I enter couples therapy in agreement with this policy.

Signature_____ Date_____

I, _____ (Client Name), hereby authorize Dr. Butch Losey, Ed.D., PCC-S to release and disclose to _____ (Partner/Spouse) all information shared, during the course of treatment, that is considered part of the couple treatment, including couples therapy sessions, individual sessions that are considered part of the couple treatment, and phone calls, emails and text messages during the authorize period identified below. The purpose of this ongoing disclosure is to provide competent treatment that allows Dr. Butch Losey, Ed.D., PCC-S to treat the couple by preventing, to the extent possible, a conflict of interest to arise where an individual's interests may not be consistent with the interests of the unit being treated.

[ ] This authorization expires 6 months from today on _____(Date).

[ ] This authorization expires less than 6 months from today on_____(Date).

Signature_____ Date_____

Role Changes

Anytime there is a clinical role change during treatment, there is added risk for the therapist and the client. Though there is not an outright ban on changing roles, many professions do, however, have a statement about role changes in their code of ethics. Consider for a moment the American Counseling Association's (2014, Standard A.6.d.) statement on role changes:

> When counselors change a role from the original or most recent contracted relationship, they obtain informed consent from the client and explain the client's right to refuse services related to the change. Examples of role changes include, but are not limited to 1. changing from individual to relationship or family counseling, or vice versa; 2. changing from an evaluative role to a therapeutic role, or vice versa; and 3. changing from a counselor to a mediator role, or vice versa. Clients must be fully informed of any anticipated consequences (e.g., financial, legal, personal, therapeutic) of counselor role changes.

A primary challenge of changing roles is the treatment alliance. A client can create a strong bond with their therapist in individual counseling,

Table 16.1 Role Changes in Couples Therapy

From couple to individual due to separation or divorce
From couple to individual due to one partner dropping out of treatment
From individual to couple due to changing treatment focus
Guest invitations

which would make it next to impossible to bring a spouse into the treatment session and have the therapist be impartial. Likewise, changing from couples therapist to individual therapist would make it difficult to return back to couples therapy and be impartial.

All role changes need to be clearly documented in the client record. The therapist should document reasons considered, arguments for and against the decision to change the role, results of consultation with other therapists and the informed consent process of the therapist.

There are several situations in which therapists will consider changing their role. Table 16.1 identifies the most common role changes.

From Couple to Individual: Due to Separation, Divorce or One Partner Dropping Out

One conclusion of couples therapy is the decision to separate or divorce. On many occasions, one partner will request to continue with the therapist in individual counseling. In many cases, the client will make the argument that they would prefer not to "start over" with another therapist. I definitely understand that, when the treatment alliance is set, it is easier to stay with the therapist than tell the backstory all over again to another therapist. What would you do? Would it make a difference if the couple was separating versus divorcing? Is there reason to notify the exiting partner that the other partner is continuing without them, in the case of separation or divorce? Most therapists believe that it is not best practice to change to individual counseling once the couple decides to separate or divorce. It is usually best to refer to another therapist, yet on occasion it may be decided that it is in the best interest of the client to change roles.

The challenge with this particular role change from couples to individual counseling is that as strange as it might sound, some couples decide to stay together after a decision to separate or divorce, and others even decide to remarry after they have divorced. If you chose to see one partner individually, ethically you would not be able to see them as a couple again, and they would lose the benefit of your service. Consider how messy that would be. First, the therapist would be a couples therapist, then an individual therapist for one partner for an extended period of time, then the couples therapist again. This scenario is high risk for malpractice or a board complaint.

Another concern is the risk of the other partner alleging an inappropriate alliance and using the individual counseling as evidence of such. It is not out of the possibility that couples may blame you for your intervention during a very difficult time in their relationship.

I believe I would be more comfortable changing the role from couples counseling to individual counseling in a situation of divorce rather than I would with an unmarried couple separating. In my experience, there have been many occasions in which unmarried couples decide to return to therapy after separating and terminating services.

If proceeding with individual counseling, I would recommend discussing the risks and benefits of making this decision, including that the role change will make it impossible to see the partners as a couple in the future. If I could, I would have this discussion with both partners.

I would make it clear that the couples chart will be closed and that either partner will have access to it and can release it to other professionals provided that both partners provide consent for it to be released. If one partner refuses the authorization to release, I will not release it. The chart for individual counseling, on the other hand, will not be accessible by the other partner.

From Individual to Couple: Due to Changing Treatment Focus

This is one of the most difficult role changes, and one that is pretty clear. There are very few reasons for changing from individual to couples therapy. The primary problem with this role change is due to the therapeutic alliance that is established in individual therapy. It is difficult to be impartial in couples therapy following any period of time with someone in individual counseling. The only exception that I consider is when I have met with an individual for one session and it is determined that couples therapy would be a better option.

I have had quite a number of couples share with me that their past couples therapy began with one partner in individual counseling and then transitioned to couples therapy. I have yet to meet one couple that had any positive things to say about the experience. I typically hear statements such as "the therapist did not seem to know what they were doing," or "the therapist was on his/her side." Some couples will ask if the role change is considered inappropriate, and then to consider that other aspects of treatment might also be inappropriate. Others will state that they had reported or had considered reporting the therapist to the state board. So, my recommendation to you is to avoid this role change altogether.

Guest Invitations

I believe guest invitations are a blending of roles that can take on some of the feeling and dynamics of couples therapy. Guest invitations typically occur in individual counseling in which the therapist or client suggests having the individual's partner attend treatment for a session or a number of sessions to support the person's individual treatment. There are many opportunities for ethical or professional concerns when inviting a guest to individual sessions. Trouble arises when (1) the therapist is unprepared for the couple dynamic that occurs in session, (2) the therapist lets the session linger without any predetermined agenda, (3) the therapist inappropriately discloses information to the guest partner, (4) the therapist continues to see both partners over an extended period of time, in essence doing couples therapy, or (5) the therapist changes the roles of individual counseling to couples counseling (this usually happens without appropriate informed consent).

Guest attendance in individual counseling is more appropriate when it is brief. I would suggest a number of guidelines for therapists considering inviting a spouse/partner to attend individual counseling (Table 16.2).

Inviting a guest to individual counseling should not be happenstance. Without goals in mind, the therapist can do more harm than good. Without clear rules, the therapist can inadvertently breach confidentiality. A guest session should be highly structured to meet a specific goal in mind.

I recommend a planning session with the individual client prior to bringing a guest into session. In the planning session, I help the client

Table 16.2 Guidelines for Guest Attendance

Schedule a planning session prior to guest attendance
Clarify goal of guest session prior to guest attendance
Clarify rules for interaction with guest
Obtain informed consent from guest at first session
Obtain authorization for release of information to speak to guest
Do not change role from individual therapist to couples therapist

identify one or two primary goals of the guest session. I am structured to the point of identifying what will occur in each 15-minute increment. I have the client identify specific topics to discuss with the guest. The plan includes what might be facilitated in session or requested of the guest.

I also want to make it very clear what the individual client is authorizing me to say and what topics are off limits. Accidental disclosers are a substantial risk with inviting a guest, particularly when inviting the spouse or partner. In this discussion, I have the client complete an authorization for release of information to talk to the guest, and I will specifically list the topic areas that are planned for discussion. I also clarify the differences between a "client" and a "guest," particularly with regard to rights and privacy.

There are a number of informed consent requirements for a guest. For example, who is a guest? A guest is usually a spouse, family member or friend who participates in therapy to assist the client. The guest is not considered to be a client, nor are they considered to be receiving treatment. Due to this, they do not have the same rights as clients.

Clients do have a right to be treated in a way that is consistent with state and federal law and have access to my privacy and client rights policies, which I provide to the guest. However, many of the privacy policy rights apply only to clients and not to someone who joins in a counseling session as a guest.

Being a guest affects how records are managed. Since guests are not receiving treatment, they will have no file and no treatment plan, and records will not be released to them. Any records that are created during the visit as a guest will be part of the file of the client. The client is able to access or release these records as needed, including any references to the attendance as a guest that are included in the file. The guest, however, does not have access to these records unless the client signs a waiver to release them to the guest.

If the guest, client or therapist believes that the guest's relationship with the client should be the main focus of treatment, then couples counseling would be suggested and a referral made to a couples therapist. The therapist could continue with individual counseling if that meets the client needs and is within their financial ability. I would caution the therapist to not make guest invitations permanent.

Domestic Violence/Partner Abuse

Approximately 10% of men and women will experience physical aggression from their partners in the context of an argument. Most, if not all, will be preceded by psychological aggression (O'Leary & Woodin, 2009). Couple therapists understand that they will at times need to work with couples in which aggression is present. Domestic violence, however, which includes force, intimidation or manipulation, is considered different by many therapists because it hinders the effectiveness of treatment. It is our ethical and professional obligation to carefully assess factors that may undermine treatment, and when partner abuse is assessed and determined, most therapists believe that it is an exclusionary criterion for couples therapy and will prefer to refer the partners to individual counseling.

Therapists struggle with knowing when to continue to treat the couple or when it is appropriate to refuse to provide couples therapy and refer one or both partners to individual therapy. According to Albert Dytch (2017), before treating an abusive couple together, they would have to meet several conditions, as outlined in Table 16.3. He emphasizes that couples therapy is appropriate when the dynamics of the relationship, not the abuse, is the focus of treatment (Dytch, 2017).

States also differ on how they require reporting of suspected domestic violence. For example, in Cincinnati where I live, Ohio therapists are not required to report domestic violence. Make sure to understand your state reporting law because it could likely create an added layer of legal, ethical and professional considerations.

Table 16.3 Parameters for Treating Abusive Couples Together

Past abuse was moderate to mild; currently, abuse is extremely mild or entirely absent.
The couple can adhere to a contract of no further abuse.
The abused partner is safe, unafraid and able to mobilize resources if needed.
Both partners are motivated for treatment out of a sincere desire to grow and change.
Both partners are willing to be accountable for their behavior, without blaming the other.
The couple can use basic communication skills in a non-manipulative manner.

Electronic Service Delivery (Telehealth)

The era of Covid-19 has taught us many things, one of which is that many therapists were not ready or not willing to offer, but capable of offering services using electronic means. Necessity changed all that. During a pleasure trip to Boulder, Colorado, in early March 2020, I began hearing about businesses closing and the subsequent run on supplies at stores. As I was leaving, stores in Boulder were running out of toilet paper. My wife was encouraging me to come home early, and the therapists at my practice (Waybridge Counseling, about 20 therapists in Cincinnati) were asking for direction about the possibility of moving to online therapy if needed. Within a few weeks, the world had changed. Within those few short weeks, my administrative team rallied, we took the practice to 100% online and it stayed that way for several months. That required us to explore and obtain the appropriate platform for counseling, review the applicable ethics and laws (which I was familiar with through my work as an ethics professor and involvement on the Ohio Counselor, Social Worker and Marriage and Family Therapist Board), train all therapists on ethics and law, develop consent documents and an assumption of risk policy and even adjust how we were processing payments.

In the United States, each state has different rules about telehealth. At the date of this writing, many states are still operating on emergency rules, which make temporary modifications to existing laws and rules to create flexibility in electronic service delivery (telehealth). What follows is how

Waybridge Counseling responded to the quick transition to telehealth and what we put into place to offer competent and ethical telehealth at the beginning of the 2020 pandemic. Our frame of reference is Ohio laws and rules and the American Counseling Association ethics. Obviously, you will consult your own state's laws and rules, but use this discussion as a guide for your practice.

Licensure Requirements

Therapists providing counseling using electronic service delivery to clients physically present in Ohio need to be licensed in Ohio. This is typical for most states. State licensing boards are generally concerned with residents in their state, so if you intend to provide counseling to a couple living or present in Ohio and you live in another state, you will be expected to have a license in Ohio. For Ohio therapists providing services in another state, they are required to comply with the laws and rules of that state.

Ohio requires an initial face-to-face meeting, which may be via video/audio electronically, to verify the identity of the electronic service delivery client. At that meeting, the therapist has a responsibility to make sure to take steps to address impostor concerns, such as by using passwords to identify the client in future electronic sessions.

Competency

To offer telehealth, you need to have competency. Competency is created by education, training and supervised experience. When the pandemic hit, we made sure that each therapist had training on the platform we were using to deliver services. Each practiced the platform and participated in a mock session for supervisors. Several training workshops on the ethics and law related to telehealth was also completed by each therapist.

We made sure that supervision continued weekly for therapists with dependent licenses with a weekly focus on electronic service delivery. We also needed to make sure that competency was created for therapists with independent licenses. To ensure competency, we developed peer-to-peer supervision triads for all therapists with independent licenses and conducted these weekly.

Informed Consent

As you can imagine, there are a number of content differences in informed consent for telehealth. Table 16.4 outlines the content that I recommend for informed consent for electronic service delivery (telehealth).

Informed consent needs to include information defining electronic service delivery and how it will be as practiced by the therapist. This includes identifying what format will be used, such as Zoom, Facetime, Doxy.me or telephone as examples. In Ohio, this consent needs to be in written form.

Even though the counseling will occur electronically, it is important for the couple to know where the therapist practices. I include my physical address and phone number. In this section, I also provide a link for couples to verify my license.

The therapists will need to identify the potential risks and benefits of offering telehealth with the use of these formats. Telehealth is not impervious to breaches or unauthorized access, and couples may have a false sense of complete security. Consent will need to indicate the possibility of breaches and how they will be managed. To create the best security possible, I indicate that I use secure practices and encrypted technology. Secure practice includes having a code word for verification when logging in, particularly if visual confirmation cannot be made. Similarly, consent should identify what to do in the event of technology failure and any alternative technology that might be used.

Table 16.4 Informed Consent Content for Electronic Service Delivery (Telehealth)

Definition of telehealth and how it is practiced by the therapist
Risk and benefits of telehealth
Limits of confidentiality and risks for breach for unauthorized access
Method for couples to verify the therapist license
Management of technology failures
Emergency procedures
Physical address of the therapist's office
Security, encryption and verification expectations

Consent needs to address emergency procedures. When the therapist is unavailable, consent will need to address who to contact. This should be a specific and identifiable person or entity, not just listing 911. When couples are not in the same locale as the therapist, the therapist should identify a local professional and provide the client with the phone number. Ohio consent requires access to the local crisis hotline telephone number and the local emergency mental health telephone number.

Therapeutic Relationship Considerations

Therapists recognize that person-to-person connection is different electronically. It is important to address potential misunderstandings that may arise from challenges with visual cues or voice intonations when communicating electronically. When telehealth is deemed ineffective by the therapist or the client, the therapist should recommend delivering services face-to-face. When the therapist is not available to provide face-to-face services, they should assist the couple in getting face-to-face sessions with another therapist.

High-Risk Clients

A high-risk client may not be appropriate for telehealth sessions. It is the therapist's responsibility to assess the couple's appropriateness for telehealth sessions. The decision to work with couples that become highly dysregulated or with one partner experiencing suicidal thought and behavior should be weighed against the decision to having a local, in-house therapist work with them.

Use of Home Office for Telehealth

As the pandemic was evolving, I set a specific policy for therapists who planned to use their home for telehealth sessions. Each clinician was required to do a mock session from their location so that they could get feedback from their supervisor on their telehealth environment. We wanted to make sure that the therapist had a private "therapy space" and that the therapist could limit the possibility of a breach, demonstrating the ability to limit intrusions and being overheard. Visual review of the therapy space also made sure that there was no accidental self-disclosure by the therapist that may occur from the client seeing a family picture or other mementos in the room.

Ethical Business Practices of Private Practice

We usually associate ethics with the clinical aspect of our work. There are also a number of ethical considerations for managing private practice. If therapists are not careful, they may unknowingly participate in unethical business practices.

Self-Referrals

Many therapists in a clinical or school setting also manage their own private practice. It may make sense that some clients in one setting might benefit from the services in the therapist's private practice, and consequently, therapists may consider referring to themselves. Therapists need to be careful in approaching self-referrals. Ethical codes suggest that therapists should not self-refer to their private practice unless the policies of a particular organization make explicit provisions for self-referrals (ACA Standard A.10.a). In such instances, the clients must be informed of other options open to them should they seek private counseling services.

Payments, Incentives and Discounts for Referrals

Therapists should not participate in fee splitting with other therapists or agencies, nor should they give or receive commissions, rebates or any other form of remuneration when referring clients for professional services (ACA Standard A.10.b; NASW Standard 2.06c).

Use of Collection Agencies

If therapists plan to use collection agencies, it is important that this policy is identified during the informed consent process (ACA Standard A.10.d.). Also, be aware that using collection agencies also increases the risk of board complaints.

Advertising and Soliciting Clients

It is important that therapists advertise their practice and credentials truthfully and not be misleading or deceptive (C.3.a). If therapists choose to use testimonials, they do not solicit them from current clients, former clients or any other persons who may be vulnerable to undue influence. They should also discuss with their clients the implications of and obtain permission for the use of any testimonial (ACA Standard C.3.b.; NASW Standard 4.07b).

Representations of Credentials

Therapists claim only the professional qualifications actually completed and correct any known misrepresentations of their qualifications by others (ACA Standard C.4.a.; NASW Standard 4.06c). Counselors do not imply doctoral-level competence when possessing a master's degree in counseling or a related field by referring to themselves as "Dr." in a counseling context when their doctorate is not in counseling or a related field. Counselors do not use "ABD" (all but dissertation) or other such terms to imply competency (ACA Standard C.4.d.).

Accepting Gifts

Therapists understand the challenges of accepting gifts from clients and recognize that in some cultures, small gifts are a token of respect and gratitude. When determining whether to accept a gift from clients, therapists take into account the therapeutic relationship, the monetary value of the gift, the client's motivation for giving the gift and the therapist's motivation for wanting to accept or decline the gift (ACA Standard A.10.f.).

Bibliography

AAMFT (2017). *Code of ethics*. Retrieved March 12, 2017, from http://aamft.org/iMIS15/AAMFT/Content/Legal_Ethics/Code_of_Ethics.aspx

American Counseling Association (2014). Code of ethics: As approved by the governing counsel.

Dytch, A. (2017). *Assessing partner abuse in couples therapy*. Retrieved March 23, 2017, from http://www.psychotherapy.net/article/couples-abuse-assessment#section-obligation-to-assess.

O'Leary, D. K., & Woodin, E. M. (2009). *Psychological and physical aggression in couples: Causes and interventions*. Washington, DC: American Psychological Association.

Weeks, G. R., Odell, M., & Methven, S. (2005). *If only I had known: Avoiding common mistakes in couples therapy*. New York: W.W. Norton & Company.

Index

Page numbers in **bold** refer to tables.

acceptance 138, 142, 144
accessibility 4, 72–73
accountability 4, 70
advocacy 70–71
affair, ending 1–2
affair partner 7–8; contact with 21–28;
  ending contact with 2, 21–23;
  grief for loss of 104–105, 108–109
aggression 14
alcohol use 10
American Association of Marriage and
  Family Therapy 159
anger 14, 111–112;
  venting 113–114, 119
Avery-Clark, C. 131

beneficence, of therapist 157
bias, initial, correction of 79
boundaries **11**
Brickell, Edie 101
Bushman, B. J. 114

cataloging 87–88
children 16–19
commitment 74–75
communication 4; management of in
  therapy 152, 160–161

compassion 57, 71–72, 84,
  95–97, 139, 144–145;
  for self 105, 107
competence, of therapist
  156–157
confidentiality 158–159
context, changes 75, 80
couples therapy: bad 150–151;
  confidentiality 158–159;
  and domestic violence/partner
  abuse 167–168, **168**; electronic
  service delivery 168–172;
  ethical business practices
  172–173; ethical considerations
  156–157; good 151–153;
  individual sessions 20, 158,
  160; informed consent 158–159;
  neutrality 157; no-secrets
  policy 159–162; role changes
  162–167, **163**; selecting therapist
  153–155
crisis stabilization 9–10

date nights 132
deception 47–48, 66
decision making, emotion-based 7
defensiveness 57, 60–61, 86

disclosure 2–4, 7, **53–55**, 108;
definition 43; preparation for 52,
64–65; self-guided 65; structured
43–66; therapist-facilitated 65;
use for therapist 66
distraction, practicing 88
divorce 14, 45
Doherty, William 150–151

emotional intelligence 124
emotional regulation 7, 59
empathy 14, 142
ending affair see affair, ending
erotic injury 122–123
erotic recovery 122–132
ERP 90–91
Exposure and Response Prevention
see ERP

false assurances 85–86
Fife, S. T. 66
forgiveness 138–139; definitions 143;
evidence-based 146–147; myths
concerning 141; process of 142–
143; seeking and obtaining 140;
of self 143; in therapy 145–148;
transformative 144–145

Gambescia, N. 66
gaslighting 32–33
Graham, Billy 82
grief 103–109; disenfranchised 103–104
growth 142
guilt 32, 111; sharing 86

health, mental: assessment 9–10;
self-care 2; taking care of 5–6
health, physical: self-care 2; taking
care of 5
honesty 69

individual therapy 20
infidelity, types of 66
informed consent 158–159,
170–171
injury, erotic see erotic injury
instability 14–15
integrity 68–69
intrusive thoughts, management of
82–92

Kretschmer, T. 79

loss 103–109; mourning 104–108
lying 29–34, 44–47; accusations of
37–39; prevention of 33; types of
29–30; see also polygraph, use to
detect lying

meaning making 142
Morrissette, Patrick 117

Nelson, Tammy 127–128, 132
neutrality, of therapist 157
non-malfeasance, of therapist 157

obsessive thoughts see intrusive
thoughts

pain 105, 107; inevitability of 57, 60
polygraph: use to detect lying 35–42;
validity of 36–37, 41
presence 73
protected time 4
psychoeducation 145
Puranam, P. 79

questions, answering 3
questions, asking 6; factual 60–61

reclaiming 128; strategies for 133–137
reconciliation 14, 139
recovery, erotic *see* erotic recovery
refocusing 88
re-scripting 91–92
retribution 14
revenge fantasies 9–10, 110–121;
    differentiating reality and fantasy
    120; disclosure 117–118;
    functions of 118; therapeutic
    techniques 119–120; treatment
    considerations 117
rumination 84, 87–88, 101, 114

scope of practice, of therapist
    156–157
self-awareness 124–125
sensate focus 126–127, 128–129;
    processing in therapy 131; stages
    and tasks of 129–131
sensual touch 125–126
sex 122; in crisis phase 128;
    disclosure about **54**; intrusive
    thoughts during 89; returning to
    relationship 123–127
sex nights, rather than date nights 132
shame 111; sharing 86
substance abuse 10
support 5; assessing quality of 19–20;
    from family and friends 13–20;
    social 106; timing 14–15

telehealth 168–172; competency 169;
    high-risk clients 171; informed

consent 170–171, **170**; licensing
    169; therapeutic relationship
    considerations 171; use of home
    office 171–172
therapy: couples *see* couples therapy;
    individual *see* individual therapy
threat assessment 9–10
time 75, 77
time, protected *see* protected time
touch, sensual *see* sensual touch
transparency 73–74
trauma 93; avoidance of 136;
    symptoms 11
triangulation 21, 28
triggering 133–135; events 4–6, 44;
    identifying and responding to
    101; management of 93–102;
    prevention of 98–99
trust **68**; building 2–4, **76–77**, 125;
    definitions 67; erosion of 78;
    rebuilding 67–81; temporal aspect
    of 79
trustworthiness 68–75, 79–80

validation 57, 84, 95–96
Vanneste, B. A. 79
Vaughan, Peggy 61–62
vulnerability 71–72, 123; in disclosure
    152; supporting 125; taking
    advantage of 18

Weeks, G. R. 66
Weiner, L. 131

Taylor & Francis Group
an **informa** business

Taylor & Francis eBooks

www.taylorfrancis.com

A single destination for eBooks from Taylor & Francis
with increased functionality and an improved user
experience to meet the needs of our customers.

90,000+ eBooks of award-winning academic content in
Humanities, Social Science, Science, Technology, Engineering,
and Medical written by a global network of editors and authors.

TAYLOR & FRANCIS EBOOKS OFFERS:

A streamlined
experience for
our library
customers

A single point
of discovery
for all of our
eBook content

Improved
search and
discovery of
content at both
book and
chapter level

REQUEST A FREE TRIAL
support@taylorfrancis.com

Routledge
Taylor & Francis Group

CRC Press
Taylor & Francis Group

For Product Safety Concerns and Information please contact our EU
representative GPSR@taylorandfrancis.com
Taylor & Francis Verlag GmbH, Kaufingerstraße 24, 80331 München, Germany

www.ingramcontent.com/pod-product-compliance
Lightning Source LLC
Chambersburg PA
CBHW050654280326
41932CB00015B/2907